SHOPPING GUIDE FOR
CARING
CONSUMERS

A GUIDE TO PRODUCTS THAT ARE NOT TESTED ON ANIMALS

cruelty free

PEOPLE FOR THE ETHICAL TREATMENT OF ANIMALS

Published by PETA
Norfolk, Va.

PETA updates this guide annually. However, we may not receive every company's updated information before going to print. Therefore, this guide is based on the most current information available at the time of publication. Some cruelty-free companies may not be included in this guide because they have not signed PETA's statement of assurance and some companies identified as those that conduct animal tests may have changed their animal-testing policies after this edition went to print. For periodically updated company information, please contact PETA or visit CaringConsumer.com.

Inclusion in this guide does not imply endorsement by PETA. We encourage consumers to shop responsibly and to question companies about their products and business practices before making any purchase.

© 2005 PETA   ISBN# 1-57067-189-3

People for the Ethical Treatment of Animals
501 Front St.
Norfolk, VA 23510
PETA.org • CaringConsumer.com

Edited by Ann Marie Dori
Proofread by Rebecca Fischer and Karen Porreca

TABLE OF **CONTENTS**

Tal Ronnen/PETA

FOREWORD

Attention, Shoppers: Welcome to PETA's *Shopping Guide for Caring Consumers!* Whether you're in love with faux leather accessories as is Persia White, our cover girl (who stars in *Girlfriends* and a PETA anti-fur ad), or looking for household cleansers that you can use with a clear conscience, this guide will hook you up with every cruelty-free product imaginable. With more than 850,000 members and supporters, PETA has grown into the largest animal rights group in the world, and the term that we popularized—"cruelty-free"—has become a household word. Today, millions of cruelty-free personal care and household cleaning products can be found under kitchen sinks and in medicine cabinets across the continent.

Having started out as a wallet-sized pamphlet listing a handful of cruelty-free companies 16 years ago, this guide has grown to list more than 500 companies, including The Body Shop, Revlon, Method Products, and Mary Kay. All the companies that you'll find in here have committed, in writing, to never testing any ingredients or finished products on animals.

Among these companies, we've designated those that are vegan—their products contain no lanolin, beeswax, or other animal ingredients. To make vegan shopping even easier, see the section that lists companies selling nonleather shoes, sporting goods, clothing, handbags, and other accessories.

To further put your wallet to work for animals, we've also included lists of health charities that do and that don't fund animal experiments, as well as a list of pet-food companies that do not conduct feeding trials on animals in laboratories.

Whether you're shopping at a gift shop, at a supermarket, or online, this guide will help you ensure that all your purchases are cruelty-free. It's caring consumers like you who are helping convince more and more companies to abandon animal tests and choose effective, humane alternatives instead. As the demand for cruelty-free products grows, so will their availability—and so will this guide!

Thank you for your compassion and for your commitment to cruelty-free living.

BLINDING BUNNIES AND POISONING MICE: INEFFECTIVE, UNNECESSARY, AND CRUEL

Every year, hundreds of thousands of rabbits, mice, rats, guinea pigs, and other animals are tortured and killed in painful product tests. Companies claim to use these inaccurate tests to determine the safety of cosmetics and other consumer products. However, these tests are widely criticized by scientists as being cruel, archaic methods that offer unreliable and often contradictory results. Furthermore, the Food and Drug Administration and the Consumer Product Safety Commission—the federal agencies that regulate cosmetics and household products, respectively—do not require that animals be used to test such products.

The notoriously cruel and unnecessary lethal-dose and Draize eye-irritancy tests, which are still being used today, date back to the 1920s. During these tests, albino rabbits are restrained, their eyelids are held open with clips, and a product or ingredient is smeared into their eyes, usually without anesthetics or analgesics. The animals are forced to endure restraint and monitoring for up to 18 days. They suffer inflammation, ulceration, hemorrhaging, and blindness. During lethal-dose tests, animals are force-fed, injected with, or forced to inhale toxic substances until a designated percentage of them die.

Modern technology has enabled hundreds of companies to use non-animal test methods such as human volunteer test subjects, *in vitro* studies, computer models, cloned human skin, tissue cultures, and extensive databases. These sophisticated, reliable, humane alternatives help ensure that cruel product tests on animals will soon be nothing more than a shameful page in our history books.

People for the Ethical Treatment of Animals (PETA) has compiled the 16th edition of the *Shopping Guide for Caring Consumers* as a part of our Caring Consumer Project.

The companies listed in this guide have signed PETA's statement of assurance or provided a statement verifying that they:

■ do not conduct animal tests on ingredients or finished products

■ do not contract with laboratories to conduct animal tests

■ will not conduct animal tests in the future

'♥' IS FOR VEGAN

Skin lotion, shaving cream, toothpaste, and lipstick—cosmetics and personal-care products like these often contain slaughterhouse byproducts or other animal-derived ingredients such as honey, silk and silk byproducts, lanolin, and substances extracted from insects or sea animals.

Many consumers who refuse to support industries that contribute to animal suffering seek out vegan products. The vegan products listed in this guide may contain plant- or mineral-based or synthetic ingredients. Companies marked with a ♥ manufacture only vegan products. Please note that most companies on our "don't test" list make at least some vegan products. Please check with the companies for more information about these products.

For a list of common animal ingredients and their alternatives, please see page 111.

COMPANIES THAT
DON'T TEST ON ANIMALS

What Types of Companies Are on the 'Don't Test' List?

The "don't test" list includes cosmetics, personal-care, and household cleaning companies only. PETA's Caring Consumer Project was founded upon the principle that no law requires that these types of products be tested on animals, so manufacturers of these products have no excuse for animal testing and should be boycotted in order to pressure them into adopting a policy that prohibits the use of animals in product tests.

This list does not include companies that manufacture only products that are required by law to be tested on animals (e.g., pharmaceuticals, automotive and garden chemicals, food additives, etc.). While PETA is opposed to all animal testing, our quarrel in this matter is with the regulatory agencies that require animal testing. Nonetheless, it is important to let representatives of companies that manufacture those products know that it is their responsibility to convince the regulatory agencies that there are better ways to determine product safety.

The "don't test" list may include companies that manufacture both products that are and products that are not required to be tested on animals, but each company that is listed here has stated that it does not conduct any animal tests that are not required by law.

LEGEND

♥ Company manufactures only vegan products—those that contain no animal ingredients. Companies without this symbol may also offer some vegan products.

■ Company is a cruelty-free subsidiary of a parent company that does not comply with the PETA statement of assurance.

🛒 Company's products can be purchased through PETA at PETAMall.com. PETA will receive 5 to 20 percent of every purchase at no extra cost to you. Please see company listings on PETAMall.com for exact percentages.

DON'T TEST ON ANIMALS

ABBA Products
7272 E. Indian School Rd.
Ste. 100
Scottsdale, AZ 85251
800-848-4475
www.abbahaircare.com
Products body care, hair care
and styling, permanent
waves, shower gel
Availability boutiques,
distributors, salons, specialty
stores
♥

Abercrombie & Fitch
6301 Fitch Path
New Albany, OH 43054
614-283-6500
888-856-4480
www.abercrombie.com
Products fragrance for men
and women, personal care
Availability Abercrombie &
Fitch stores

Abra Therapeutics
10365 Hwy. 116
Forestville, CA 95436
707-869-0761
800-745-0761
www.abratherapeutics.com
Products aromatherapy, baby
bathing supply, bubble bath,
hypo-allergenic skin care for
men and women, sun care
Availability boutiques, health
food stores, mail order, spas,
specialty stores
♥

**Advanage Wonder
Cleaner**
16615 S. Halsted St.
Harvey, IL 60426
708-333-7644
800-323-6444
www.wondercleaner.com
Products all-purpose cleaner
Availability independent sales
representatives, mail order
♥

Afrumos
P.O. Box 90613
Portland, OR 97290
503-715-3127
www.afrumos.com
Products body care,
cosmetics, foot care, hypo-
allergenic skin care
Availability boutiques, mail
order, salons, Web site

Alba Botanica
1105 Industrial Ave.
Petaluma, CA 94952
707-347-1200
800-227-5120
www.avalonorganics.com
Products deodorant, hair
care and styling, self-tanning
lotion, shaving cream, shower
gel, skin care for men and
women, soap,
sun care
Availability boutiques,
cooperatives, drugstores,
health food stores, mail
order, specialty stores, Web
site

**Alexandra Avery Purely
Natural**
4717 S.E. Belmont
Portland, OR 97215
503-236-5926
800-669-1863
www.alexandraavery.com
Products aromatherapy,
fragrance for men and
women, lubricants, shaving
supply, skin care, soap,
sun care
Availability boutiques,
cooperatives, health food
stores, mail order, specialty
stores

Alima Cosmetics, Inc.
P.O. Box 22624
Portland, OR 97269
503-659-0033
www.alimacosmetics.com
Products cosmetics
Availability Web site

Allens Naturally
P.O. Box 514, Dept. M
Farmington, MI 48332-0514
248-449-7708
800-352-8971
www.allensnaturally.com
Products all-purpose cleaner,
dish detergent, fabric
softener, fruit and vegetable
wash, laundry detergent
Availability cooperatives,
health food stores, mail
order
♥

Almay (Revlon)
625 Madison Ave.
New York, NY 10022
212-572-5000
www.almay.com
Products cosmetics,
deodorant, hypo-allergenic
skin care for men and
women, lip care, nail care,
sun care
Availability drugstores,
supermarkets

Aloette Cosmetics
4900 Highland Pkwy.
Smyrna, GA 30082
800-ALOETTE
www.aloette.com
Products cosmetics,
fragrance for men and
women, hair care and styling,
nail care, self-tanning lotion,
shower gel, skin care for
men and women, sun care
Availability independent sales
representatives

Aloe Up
5821 E. Harrison Ave.
Harlingen, TX 78550-1811
210-428-0081
800-950-2563
www.aloeup.com
Products body care, essential
oils, hair care, hypo-allergenic
skin care for men and
women, insect repellant, lip
care, skin care, sunburn relief,
sun care, toiletries
Availability boutiques,
drugstores, health food
stores, mail order, specialty
stores, supermarkets

Aloe Vera of America
9660 Dilworth Rd.
Dallas, TX 75243
214-343-5700
Products aromatherapy,
bathing supply, companion
animal care, cosmetics, dental
hygiene, deodorant, hair
care, household supply,
laundry detergent, lip care,
shaving supply, skin care,
soap, vegan makeup brushes,
vitamins
Availability independent sales
representatives

**Amazon Premium
Products**
3260 Keith Bridge Rd., #308
Cumming, GA 30041
678-513-2900
800-832-5645
Products all-purpose cleaner,
bathroom cleaner, furniture
polish, stain remover
Availability hardware stores,
mail order
♥

American Beauty
767 Fifth Ave.
New York, NY 10153
866-352-8337
www.americanbeautycosmetics.
com
Products cosmetics, skin care
Availability Kohl's
department stores, Web site

American International
2220 Gaspar Ave.
Los Angeles, CA 90040
213-728-2999
www.aiibeauty.com
Products cosmetics,
depilatory, hair care, hair
color, nail care, skin care,
toiletries
Availability beauty supply
stores, boutiques, discount
department stores,
drugstores, health food
stores, specialty stores,
supermarkets

American Safety Razor
1 Razor Blade Ln.
Verona, VA 24482
540-248-8000
800-445-9284
www.asrco.com
Products razors, shaving
cream
Availability boutiques,
department stores, discount
department stores,
drugstores, health food
stores, mail order, specialty
stores, supermarkets

**America's Finest
Products Corporation**
1639 Ninth St.
Santa Monica, CA 90404
310-450-6555
800-482-6555
Products all-purpose cleaner,
concrete cleaner, Elbow
Grease, fine washables
detergent, household supply,
liquid cleaner, stain remover,
water softener
Availability drugstores, mail
order, supermarkets
♥

Amitée
(Advanced Research Labs)
151 Kalmus Dr., Ste. H3
Costa Mesa, CA 92626
714-556-1028
800-966-6960
www.amitee.com
Products hair care
Availability beauty supply
stores, drugstores,
supermarkets

Ancient Formulas
638 W. 33rd St. N.
Wichita, KS 67204
316-838-5600
800-543-3026
Products acne treatment,
dental hygiene, herbal
supplements, holistic health
care, sleeping aids
Availability cooperatives,
drugstores, health food
stores, mail order, physicians

COMPANIES THAT
DON'T TEST ON ANIMALS

**Andrea International
Industries**
2220 Gaspar Ave.
Los Angeles, CA 90040
213-728-2999
www.aiibeauty.com
Products bathing supply,
depilatory, foot care, skin
care
Availability boutiques,
discount department stores,
drugstores, mass retailers,
specialty stores,
supermarkets

**Anna Marie's
Aromatherapy and
Massage**
108 Allan Ln.
Butler, PA 16001
724-282-6469
www.annieallan.ameranet.com
Products aromatherapy, baby
care, bathing supply, body
care, companion animal care,
fragrance for women, healing
salve, insect repellent, lip
care, massage oil, skin care
Availability Anna Marie's
Aromatherapy store, Web
site

The Apothecary Shoppe
5940 S.W. Hood Ave.
Portland, OR 97239
503-244-0726
800-487-8839
www.herbed.com
Products air freshener,
aromatherapy, candles,
herbal supplements
Availability mail order,
Web site

Aramis
767 Fifth Ave.
New York, NY 10153
212-572-3700
www.elcompanies.com
Products bathing supply,
deodorant, fragrance for
men and women, hair care,
razors, shaving supply, skin
care for men and women,
soap, sun care, toiletries
Availability department
stores, specialty stores

Arbonne International
9420 Jeronimo
Irvine, CA 92618
949-770-2610
800-ARBONNE
www.arbonne.com
Products acne treatment,
anti-aging treatments,
aromatherapy, baby care,
cosmetics, dandruff
shampoo, hair care, herbal
supplements, hypo-allergenic
skin care for men and
women, lip care, massage
oil/lotion, nutritional bars and
shakes, progesterone cream,
self-tanning lotion, shaving
cream, shower gel, skin care
for men and women, sun
care, vitamins
Availability independent sales
representatives
🛒

Ardell International
2220 Gaspar Ave.
Los Angeles, CA 90040
213-728-2999
www.aiibeauty.com
Products body care,
depilatory, hair color
Availability boutiques,
discount department stores,
drugstores, specialty stores,
supermarkets

Arganat, Inc.
2402 Bedford
Montréal, QC H3S 2W9
Canada
514-941-6955
www.arganat.net
Products bath oil, body care,
dental hygiene, hypo-
allergenic skin care
Availability health food
stores, Web site

Aroma Crystal Therapy
155 Rainbow Rd.
Salt Spring Island, BC
V8K 2M3
Canada
250-537-9211
877-537-9211
www.aromacrystal.com
Products acne treatment,
aromatherapy, body care,
companion animal care, first
aid, hair care, holistic health
care, lip care, scar gel,
shower gel, skin care
Availability Aroma Crystal
Therapy store, department
stores, drugstores, health
food stores, mail order, Web
site
♥ 🛒

COMPANIES THAT
DON'T TEST ON ANIMALS

Aromaland
1326 Rufina Cir.
Santa Fe, NM 87505
505-438-0402
800-933-5267
www.buyaromatherapy.com
Products air freshener,
aromatherapy, candles,
fragrance for women, hair
care, massage oil, nail care,
shower gel, skin care, soap
Availability bookstores,
health food stores, salons,
spas, Web site

Aromaleigh, Inc.
301 Central Ave., #325
Hilton Head, SC 29926
843-681-4716
www.aromaleigh.com
Products aromatherapy,
cosmetics, lip care
Availability Web site

Aroma Vera
5310 Beethoven St.
Los Angeles, CA 90066
310-280-0407
800-669-9514
www.aromavera.com
Products acne treatment,
air freshener, aromatherapy,
bubble bath, candles,
fragrance for men and
women, hair care, massage
oil/lotion, shower gel, skin
care for men and women,
soap
Availability Aroma Vera
stores, boutiques, health food
stores, mail order, salons,
spas, specialty stores

Astonish Industries, Inc.
Business Pk.
423 Commerce Ln., Unit 2
West Berlin, NJ 08091
609-753-7078
800-530-5385
Products air freshener, all-
purpose cleaner, bathroom
cleaner, bleach, car care,
carpet cleaner, cream
cleanser, dish detergent,
laundry detergent, oven
cleaner, stain remover, toilet
cleaner
Availability mail order,
specialty stores
♥

At Last Naturals
401 Columbus Ave.
Valhalla, NY 10595
914-479-0900
800-527-8123
www.alast.com
Products acne treatment,
herbal supplements,
nonprescription therapy,
progesterone cream, soap
Availability drugstores, health
food stores, mail order

Aubrey Organics, Inc.
4419 N. Manhattan Ave.
Tampa, FL 33614
813-877-4186
800-AUBREYH
www.aubrey-organics.com
Products aftershave lotion,
air freshener, all-purpose
cleaner, baby bathing supply,
bathroom cleaner,
companion animal care,
cosmetics, deodorant,
fragrance for men and
women, hair care and styling,
hair color, insect repellent, lip
care, make-up remover,
mouthwash, shaving cream,
skin care, soap, sun care,
toothpaste
Availability health food
stores, web site

Aunt Bee's Skin Care
P.O. Box 2678
Rancho de Taos, NM 87577
505-737-0522
888-233-2256
Products aromatherapy,
cosmetics, lip care,
skin care, soap, sun care
Availability drugstores, health
food stores, supermarkets

Aura Cacia
P.O. Box 299
3021 78th St.
Norway, IA 52318
800-437-3301
www.auracacia.com
Products aromatherapy,
bathing supply, fragrance for
men and women, hair styling,
lip care, massage oil/lotion,
skin care, soap
Availability boutiques,
cooperatives, discount
department stores,
drugstores, health food
stores, mail order, specialty
stores

**Auromère Ayurvedic
Imports**
2621 W. Hwy. 12
Lodi, CA 95242
800-735-4691
www.auromere.com
Products ayurvedic supply,
bathing supply, dental
hygiene, incense, massage oil,
skin care for men and
women, soap
Availability health food
stores
♥

Austin Rose
177-F Riverside Ave.
Newport Beach, CA 92663
714-662-5465
800-292-6339
www.austinrose.com
Products air freshener,
companion animal care
Availability boutiques,
cooperatives, distributors,
drugstores, health food
stores, mail order, specialty
stores, supermarkets, Web
site
♥

**The Australasian
College of Health
Sciences**
5940 S.W. Hood Ave.
Portland, OR 97239
503-244-0726
800-487-8839
www.herbed.com
Products air freshener,
aromatherapy, bathing supply,
candles, herbal supplements,
soap
Availability mail order, Web
site

Autumn Harp
61 Pine St.
Bristol, VT 05443
802-453-4807
www.autumnharp.com
Products cosmetics, fragrance
for women, nonprescription
therapy, personal care
Availability cooperatives,
department stores,
drugstores, health food
stores, mail order,
supermarkets

**Avalon Organic
Botanicals**
1105 Industrial Ave.
Petaluma, CA 94952
707-347-1200
800-227-5120
www.avalonorganics.com
Products body care,
deodorant, hair care, hypo-
allergenic skin care for men
and women, shaving cream,
shower gel, soap, sun care
Availability boutiques, health
food stores, mail order,
specialty stores, Web site

Aveda Corporation
767 Fifth Ave.
New York, NY 10153
800-AVEDA-24
www.aveda.com
Products aftershave lotion,
air freshener, aromatherapy,
candles, cosmetics,
deodorant, ethnic personal
care, hair care and styling,
hypo-allergenic skin care, lip
care, massage oil/lotion,
shaving cream, shower gel,
soap, sun care
Availability Aveda stores,
environmentally friendly
stores, health care facilities,
salons, spas

Avigal Henna
45-49 Davis St.
Long Island City, NY 11101
718-361-3123
800-722-1011
Products henna hair color
Availability health food
stores, salons, specialty stores
♥

Avon
1251 Ave. of the Americas
New York, NY 10020
212-282-7000
800-858-8000
www.avon.com
Products acne treatment,
baby bathing supply, bubble
bath, candles, cosmetics,
dandruff shampoo,
deodorant, ethnic personal
care, fragrance for men and
women, hair care and styling,
hypo-allergenic skin care for
men and women, insect
repellent, lip care, nail care,
shower gel, soap, sun care
Availability distributors, mail
order, Web site

A Wild Texas Soap Bar
21407 Union Lee Church
Rd.
Manor, TX 78653
512-272-4058
www.awildtexassoapbar.com
Products body care, soap
Availability boutiques, Web
site

Ayurherbal Corporation
1100 Lotus Dr.
Silver Lake, WI 53170
414-889-8569
Products air freshener, dental
hygiene, fragrance for men
and women, household
supply, incense, toiletries
Availability boutiques,
cooperatives, drugstores,
health food stores, mail
order, specialty stores
♥

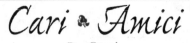

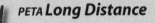

Ayurveda Holistic Center
82A Bayville Ave.
Bayville, NY 11709
516-628-8200
www.ayurveda.com
Products aromatherapy, companion animal care, hair care, herbal supplements, lip care, massage oil/lotion, nonprescription therapy, soap, sun care, toothpaste
Availability Ayurveda Holistic Center stores, health food stores
♥

Bare Escentuals
425 Bush St., 3rd Fl.
San Francisco, CA 94108
415-288-3500
800-227-3990
www.bareescentuals.com
Products aromatherapy, bubble bath, candles, cosmetics, deodorant, fragrance for women, hair care, hypo-allergenic skin care, massage oil/lotion, nail care, shaving supply, shower gel, soap
Availability Bare Escentuals stores, boutiques, department stores, mail order, specialty stores

Basis (Beiersdorf)
BDF Plz.
360 Martin Luther King Dr.
Norwalk, CT 06856-5529
203-853-8008
www.beiersdorf.com
Products skin care, soap
Availability drugstores, supermarkets

Bath & Body Works
7 Limited Pkwy. E.
Reynoldsburg, OH 43068
614-856-6585
800-395-1001
www.bathandbodyworks.com
Products air freshener, aromatherapy, baby care, bubble bath, deodorant, fragrance for women, hair care, hypo-allergenic skin care, insect repellent, lip care, nail care, shaving supply, shower gel, soap, sun care
Availability Bath & Body Works stores

Bath Island
469 Amsterdam Ave.
New York, NY 10024
212-787-9415
877-234-3657
www.bathisland.com
Products air freshener, aromatherapy, baby bathing supply, bubble bath, companion animal shampoo, dandruff shampoo, fragrance for women, hair care, household supply, lip care, massage oil/lotion, nail care, shower gel, skin care, soap, sun care, toothbrushes, toothpaste
Availability Bath Island store, mail order, Web site

Bath Petals, Inc.
830 S. Hill St., #850
Los Angeles, CA 90014
888-228-4738
www.bathpetals.com
Products aromatherapy, body care, body oil, bath salts, candles, shower gel
Availability spas, Web site

Baudelaire
P.O. Box 10116
Swanzey, NH 03446-0116
603-352-9234
800-327-2324
www.baudelairesoaps.com
Products aftershave lotion, aromatherapy, fragrance for men and women, hair care, lip care, shower gel, skin care, soap, sun care
Availability drugstores, gift boutiques, health food stores

BeautiControl
2121 Midway Rd.
Carrollton, TX 75006
972-458-0601
www.beauticontrol.com
Products acne treatment, bubble bath, cosmetics, fragrance for men and women, hypo-allergenic skin care, nail care, shower gel, soap, sun care, vitamins
Availability distributors

Beauty Naturally
P.O. Box 4905
850 Stanton Rd.
Burlingame, CA 94010
650-697-1845
800-432-4323
www.beautynaturally.com
Products acne treatment, hypo-allergenic skin care for men and women
Availability health food stores, mail order, Web site

Beauty Without Cruelty
1340-G Industrial Ave.
Petaluma, CA 94952
707-763-0663
888-674-2344
www.beautywithoutcruelty.
com
Products cosmetics, hair care
and styling, hypo-allergenic
skin care for men and
women, sun care
Availability boutiques, health
food stores, mail order,
specialty stores, Web site

Beiersdorf
Wilton Corporate Center
187 Danbury Rd.
Wilton, CT 06897
203-853-8008
www.beiersdorf.com
Products body care, skin
care, soap
Availability drugstores,
supermarkets

Belisama Bodyworks
58 Church St.
Saratoga Springs, NY 12866
518-248-0090
www.belisamabodyworks.com
Products aromatherapy, bath
salts, body care, deodorant,
hair care, insect repellant, lip
care, massage oil, shower gel,
skin care
Availability Belisama
Bodyworks store, mail order,
Web site

Berol (Sanford)
2711 Washington Blvd.
Bellwood, IL 60104
708-547-5525
800-438-3703
www.sanfordcorp.com
Products ink, office supply,
writing instruments
Availability department
stores, drugstores, mail order,
office supply stores,
supermarkets

Better Botanicals
335 Victory Dr.
Herndon, VA 20170
703-481-3300
888-BB-HERBS
www.betterbotanicals.com
Products aromatherapy, hair
care, lip care, massage
oil/lotion, skin care for men
and women, soap
Availability boutiques, health
food stores, spas, Web site

Beverly Hills Cold Wax
P.O. Box 600476
San Diego, CA 92160
619-283-0880
800-833-0889
Products wax depilatory
Availability beauty supply
stores, health food stores,
mail order, salons

BioFilm
3121 Scott St.
Vista, CA 92083
619-727-9030
800-848-5900
www.biofilm.com
Products lubricants
Availability drugstores
♥

Biogime International, Inc.
25602 I-45 N., Ste. 106
Spring, TX 77386
281-298-2607
800-338-8784
www.biogimeskincare.com
Products bubble bath, hair
care, hypo-allergenic skin
care for men and women,
lotions, shower gel, sun care
Availability independent sales
representatives, mail order
♥

BI-O-KLEEN
P.O. Box 820689
Vancouver, WA 98682
800-477-0188
360-576-0064
www.bi-o-kleen.com
Products all-purpose cleaner,
bleach, carpet cleaner, dish
detergent, fruit and
vegetable wash, household
supply, laundry detergent,
stain remover
Availability drugstores, health
food stores, mail order,
supermarkets, Web site
♥ ⌐

Biokosma
(Caswell-Massey)
121 Fieldcrest Ave.
Edison, NJ 08818-6161
800-326-0500
www.caswell-massey.com
Products bathing supply,
hypo-allergenic skin care
Availability mail order,
specialty stores

Bio Pac
584 Pinto Ct.
Incline Village, NV 89451
800-225-2855
www.bio-pac.com
Products all-purpose cleaner,
automatic dishwashing
detergent, bathroom cleaner,
bleach, dish detergent, fabric
softener, glass cleaner, hair
care, laundry detergent, soap,
stain remover, toilet cleaner
Availability health food
stores
♥

Biotone
4757 Old Cliffs Rd.
San Diego, CA 92120
619-582-0027
www.biotone.com
Products aromatherapy, body
care, essential oil, massage
oil/lotion
Availability boutiques,
independent sales
representatives, mail order,
massage therapists, specialty
stores

Blooming Lotus
130 W. 18th St.
Kansas City, MO 64108
816-444-4735
866-444-4735
Products aromatherapy, baby
care, bathing supply,
household supply, insect
repellent, lip care, massage
oil/lotion, skin care, soap
Availability boutiques, health
food stores, mail order

Bobbi Brown
767 Fifth Ave.
New York, NY 10153
212-572-4200
www.bobbibrown.com
Products baby bathing
supply, cosmetics, ethnic
personal care, fragrance for
women, lip care, nail care,
self-tanning lotion, skin care
Availability department
stores, Web site

Body Bistro
P.O. Box 5788
Beverly Hills, CA 90209-
5778
818-487-8181
www.bodybistro.com
Products aromatherapy,
shower gel, skin care, soap
Availability department
stores, mail order, Web site

Body Encounters
230 N. Maple Ave.
Crispin Square
Marlton, NJ 08053
www.bodyencounters.com
Products aromatherapy,
candles, massage oil/lotion,
skin care for men and
women
Availability Body Encounters
store, mail order, Web site

Bodyography
1641 16th St.
Santa Monica, CA 90404
310-399-2886
800-642-2639
www.bodyography.com
Products cosmetics
Availability beauty supply
stores, salons

The Body Shop
5036 One World Way
Wake Forest, NC 27587
919-554-4900
www.thebodyshop.com
Products air freshener,
aromatherapy, baby care,
bathing supply, cosmetics,
dental hygiene, deodorant,
fragrance for women, hair
care, hair color, lip care, nail
care, razors, shaving supply,
skin care, soap, sun care,
toiletries, toothbrushes
Availability The Body Shop
stores, mail order

Body Time
1101 Eighth St., Ste. 100
Berkeley, CA 94710
510-524-0216
888-649-2639
www.bodytime.com
Products aftershave lotion,
aromatherapy, baby bathing
supply, candles, fragrance for
men and women, hair care,
massage oil, shaving supply,
shower gel, skin care for
men and women, soap, sun
care
Availability Body Time stores,
mail order

**Bon Ami/Faultless
Starch**
1025 W. Eighth St.
Kansas City, MO 64101-1200
816-842-1230
www.bonami.com
Products air freshener, all-
purpose cleaner, copper and
stainless-steel cleaner, glass
cleaner, laundry detergent,
powdered cleanser, starch,
wrinkle remover, antiaging
treatment
Availability cooperatives,
drugstores, health food
stores, supermarkets

Bonne Bell
1006 Crocker Rd.
Westlake, OH 44145
216-221-0800
www.bonnebell.com
Products acne treatment,
cosmetics, deodorant,
fragrance for men and
women, lip care, nail care,
self-tanning lotion, shower
gel, skin care, soap, sun care
Availability department stores,
drugstores, supermarkets

Börlind of Germany, Inc.
P.O. Box 130
New London, NH 03257-0130
603-763-6400
800-447-7024
www.borlind.com
Products acne treatment,
anti-aging treatment,
cosmetics, lip care, skin care,
sun care
Availability boutiques, health
food stores, salons, spas,
specialty stores

Boscia
811 Kaiser Ave.
Irvine, CA 92614
888-635-8884
www.boscia.net
Products skin care
Availability mail order, Web site
♥

Botanics Skin Care
P.O. Box 384
Ukiah, CA 95482
707-462-6141
800-800-6141
Products fragrance for men
and women, hair care,
hypo-allergenic skin care,
shower gel
Availability boutiques,
cooperatives, department
stores, health food stores,
mail order, specialty stores

Brocato International
3939 E. 46th St.
Minneapolis, MN 55406
800-243-0275
www.brocatoamerica.com
Products hair care and
styling, permanent waves
Availability boutiques, salons,
specialty stores

Bronzo Sensualé
P.O. Box 546225
Miami Beach, FL 33154
305-861-5100
800-991-2226
www.bronzosensuale.com
Products aromatherapy,
baby bathing supply, hypo-
allergenic skin care for men
and women, lip care,
lubricants, self-tanning lotion,
sun care
Availability boutiques,
drugstores, health food
stores, mail order, spas,
specialty stores
♥

Brookside Soap Company
1309 Bonneville Ave., Ste. A
Snohomish, WA 98290-2065
360-568-5938
800-243-0275
www.brooksidesoap.com
Product companion animal
care, soap
Availability health food
stores
♥

Bug-Off
P.O. Box 1881
Burlington, VT 05402-1881
802-860-1680
Products insect repellent
Availability cooperatives,
environmentally friendly
stores, health food stores,
mail order, sporting goods
stores, veterinarians
♥

Bugs B Wear
4535 Hodgson Rd., Ste. 300
Shoreview, MN 55126
651-429-6269
www.bugsbwear.com
Products insect repellent
Availability department
stores, gift boutiques, mail
order, Web site

Bumble and bumble
146 E. 56th St.
New York, NY 10022
212-521-6500
800-7-BUMBLE
www.bumbleandbumble.com
Products hair care and
styling, hair color
Availability Bumble and
bumble salon, salons

Caeran
5556-5th Line Eramosa
RR#1
Rockwood, ON N0B 2K0
Canada
519-751-0513
800-563-2974
www.caeran.com
Products all-purpose cleaner,
automatic dishwashing
detergent, bathroom cleaner,
bubble bath, car care, carpet
cleaner, deodorant, fabric
softener, hair care, hypo-
allergenic skin care, laundry
detergent, lip care,
mouthwash, shower gel,
soap, sun care, vitamins
Availability boutiques, health
food stores, independent
sales representatives, mail
order, specialty stores

Calaby Creations
679 Meadowview Dr.
Centerville, OH 45459
937-545-8496
www.calabycreations.com
Products soap
Availability Web site

California North
P.O. Box 2820
Schoonmaker Pt. Marina
Sausalito, CA 94966-1633
415-331-1633
www.californianorth.com
Products aftershave lotion,
air freshener, fragrance for
men and women, hair care,
self-tanning lotion, shaving
cream, skin care, soap, sun
care
Availability drugstores, mail
order, Web site

California SunCare
10877 Wilshire Blvd.
12th Fl.
Los Angeles, CA 90024
800-SUN-CARE
www.caltan.com
Products self-tanning lotion,
skin care for men and
women, sun care
Availability salons

CamoCare
61 Broadway, Ste. 1310
New York, NY 10006
212-292-1550
800-CAMOCARE
www.camocare.com
Products body care, hair
care, skin care
Availability health food
stores, mail order

**Candy Kisses Natural
Lip Balm**
417 Fifth Ave., 9th Fl.
New York, NY 10016
212-726-0714
www.candykisses.com
Products lip care
Availability discount
department stores,
drugstores, mail order,
supermarkets
♥

Carina Corporation
304 Kennard Ave.
N. Vancouver, BC V7J 3J8
Canada
604-985-5120
www.carinaorganics.com
Products hair care
Availability Carina Supply
stores, mail order, salons,
Web site

Carlson Laboratories
15 College Dr.
Arlington Heights, IL 60004
847-255-1600
888-234-5656
www.carlsonlabs.com
Products hair care, skin care,
soap, vitamins
Availability health food
stores

Carma Laboratories
5801 W. Airways Ave.
Franklin, WI 53132
414-421-7707
www.carma-labs.com
Products cold sore medicine,
lip care, nonprescription
therapy, sun care
Availability department
stores, drugstores, health
food stores, supermarkets

**Carrot Tree Soaps &
Essentials**
8368 Serenity Ln.
Pulaski, WI 54162
920-822-2965
866-260-6964
www.carrottreesoaps.com
Products aromatherapy, body
care, massage oil, soap
Availability Web site

Caswell-Massey
121 Fieldcrest Ave.
Edison, NJ 08818-6161
732-512-3225
800-326-0500
www.caswellmassey.com
Products aftershave lotion,
baby bathing supply, bubble
bath, deodorant, fragrance
for men and women, hair
care, lip care, nail care,
razors, shaving cream,
shower gel, skin care, soap,
toothbrushes, toothpaste
Availability boutiques,
Caswell-Massey stores,
department stores, discount
department stores,
drugstores, health food
stores, mail order, specialty
stores, Web site

Celestial Body, Inc.
21298 Pleasant Hill Rd.
Boonville, MO 65233
660-882-6858
800-882-6858
www.celestialbody.com
Products acne treatment,
aromatherapy, bathing supply,
hypo-allergenic skin care for
men and women, soap
Availability boutiques,
cooperatives, health food
stores, independent sales
representatives, mail order,
specialty stores

Chanel
9 W. 57th St.
New York, NY 10019
212-688-5055
800-550-0005
www.chanel.com
Products bathing supply,
cosmetics, deodorant,
fragrance for men and
women, nail care, skin care
for men and women, soap,
sun care, toiletries
Availability Chanel stores,
department stores

10 REASONS TO CHOOSE AUBREY ORGANICS®

1. A NATURAL TRADITION FOR OVER 35 YEARS
All Aubrey Organics® products are 100% natural, with no petrochemicals of any kind.

2. QAI CERTIFIED ORGANIC PROCESSOR
Aubrey Organics® was the first hair and skin care manufacturer to be certified as an organic processor, in October 1994, by Quality Assurance International of San Diego, CA— an important step towards guaranteeing the purity and quality of our products. We use certified organic ingredients whenever possible in our 100% natural formulas.

3. NATURAL IS BETTER FOR YOUR HAIR AND SKIN
Long-term effects of harsh petrochemicals on the body and the environment are still unknown. We are committed to using 100% natural ingredients that have a proven track record of safety and efficacy.

4. THE MOST COMPLETE BODY CARE LINE
We offer the most extensive hair, skin and body care line in the natural personal care products industry—something for the entire family!

5. 100% CUSTOMER SATISFACTION
We stand behind our products with a 100% money-back guarantee. If your customers are not completely satisfied with a product, simply return it for a refund.

6. ENVIRONMENTALLY SAFE PRODUCTS
Our products are safe for the environment because they don't introduce petrochemicals into the air, land or water—they are completely biodegradable. And we use recyclable (HDPE) plastic bottles in as much of our packaging as possible.

7. WORLD HERBAL TRADITIONS
We purchase herbal ingredients for fair market value around the world and use them in all-natural formulas—the most sustainable and ethical use of these fine ingredients.

8. HANDCRAFTED PRODUCTS
Our products are handmade in quantities of 50 gallons or less—by people instead of machines, and formulated in small batches for the freshest product possible.

9. AFFORDABLE QUALITY
At Aubrey Organics® we believe a product is only as good as its ingredients. That's why we source only the highest quality natural and certified organic ingredients to bring you the finest personal care products at the best price.

10. NO ANIMAL TESTING
We do not test on animals, nor do we accept animal testing data as proof of an ingredient's safety or effectiveness.

Look for us in better health food stores everywhere, or call 1-800-237-4270 to order.

Christine Valmy, Inc.
285 Change Bridge Rd.
Pine Brook, NJ 07058
973-575-1050
800-526-5057
www.christinevalmy.com
Products aromatherapy,
hypo-allergenic skin care,
shaving supply
Availability independent
distributors, salons

Chuckles (Farmavita)
P.O. Box 5126
Manchester, NH 03109
603-669-4228
800-221-3496
www.sukesha.com
Products hair care and
styling, hair color
Availability salons

CiCi Cosmetics
215 N. Eucalyptus Ave.
Inglewood, CA 90301
310-680-9696
800-869-1224
www.cicicosmetics.com
Products cosmetics,
lip care
Availability boutiques,
discount department stores,
drugstores, mail order,
specialty stores

Cinema Secrets
4400 Riverside Dr.
Burbank, CA 91505
818-846-0579
www.cinemasecrets.com
Products cosmetics, skin
care, theatrical makeup
Availability beauty supply
stores, Cinema Secrets
stores, costume/novelty
stores, mail order, salons

Citra-Solv, LLC
188 Shadow Lake Rd.
Ridgefield, CT 06877-1032
203-778-0881
800-343-6588
www.citrasolv.com
Products air freshener, all-
purpose cleaner, automatic
dishwashing detergent, baby
care, bathing supply, car care,
carpet cleaner, dish detergent,
drain cleaner, furniture polish,
glass cleaner, laundry
detergent, oven cleaner, soap,
stain remover
Availability boutiques,
cooperatives, discount
department stores, health
food stores, mail order,
specialty stores, supermarkets
♥

Citré Shine
1063 McGaw, Ste. 100
Irvine, CA 92614
949-794-5500
www.citreshine.com
Products hair care and
styling
Availability beauty supply
stores, drugstores,
supermarkets
■

Clarins of Paris
110 E. 59th St.
New York, NY 10022
212-980-1800
www.clarins.com
Products aftershave lotion,
bubble bath, cosmetics,
deodorant, fragrance for
women, hair care, hypo-
allergenic skin care for men
and women, nail care, self-
tanning lotion, shaving cream,
shower gel, sun care
Availability boutiques,
department stores, specialty
stores

Clear Conscience
P.O. Box 17855
Arlington, VA 22216-1785
703-527-7566
800-595-9592
www.clearconscience.com
Products contact lens
solutions
Availability cooperatives,
health food stores, mail
order, supermarkets, Web
site
♥ ☷

Clear Logix
1063 McGaw, Ste. 100
Irvine, CA 92614
949-794-5500
www.citreshine.com
Products skin care
Availability beauty supply
stores, drugstores,
supermarkets
■

**Clearly Natural
Products**
1340 N. McDowell Blvd.
Petaluma, CA 94954
707-762-5815
www.clearlynaturalsoaps.com
Products glycerin soap
Availability drugstores, health
food stores, supermarkets,
Web site
♥

COMPANIES THAT
DON'T TEST ON ANIMALS

Clear Vue Products
P.O. Box 567
417 Canal St.
Lawrence, MA 01842
978-794-3100
www.sunpointinc.com
Products glass cleaner
Availability mail order,
supermarkets
♥

Clientele
14101 N.W. Fourth St.
Sunrise, FL 33325
954-845-9500
800-327-4660
www.clientele.org
Products acne treatment,
bathing supply, cosmetics,
fragrance for men and
women, hair care, hypo-
allergenic skin care for men
and women, lip care, nail
care, nail polish remover,
soap, sun care, theatrical
makeup, toiletries, vitamins
Availability boutiques,
department stores, mail
order, specialty stores

Clinique Laboratories
767 Fifth Ave.
New York, NY 10153
212-572-3800
www.clinique.com
Products acne treatment,
aftershave lotion, cosmetics,
deodorant, ethnic personal
care, fragrance for men and
women, hair care, hypo-
allergenic skin care, nail care,
self-tanning lotion, shaving
cream, sun care
Availability department
stores, specialty stores

Collective Wellbeing
P.O. Box 2046
Irwindale, CA 91706
800-896-4649
www.collectivewellbeing.com
Products bathing supply,
body care, dandruff
shampoo, foot care, hair
care, hypo-allergenic skin
care, lip care, lubricants, soap
Availability health food
stores, mail order, Web site

Colonial Dames
6820 E. Watcher St.
Commerce, CA 90040
323-773-6441
800-774-6441
www.colonial-dames.com
Products body care, hair
care, skin care, soap, sun care
Availability drugstores, health
food stores, mail order,
supermarkets, Web site
♥

Color Me Beautiful
14900 Conference Center
Dr.
Chantilly, VA 20151
703-471-6400
800-COLORME
www.colormebeautiful.com
Products cosmetics,
fragrance for women, self-
tanning lotion, skin care for
men and women, sun care
Availability boutiques,
department stores,
drugstores, independent
sales representatives, mail
order, specialty stores

Color My Image
5025B Backlick Rd.
Annandale, VA 22003
703-354-9797
www.colormyimage.com
Products body care,
cosmetics, hypo-allergenic
skin care, lip care, makeup
remover, theatrical makeup
Availability Color My Image
stores, mail order

**Columbia Cosmetics
Manufacturing**
1661 Timothy Dr.
San Leandro, CA 94577
510-562-5900
800-824-3328
www.columbiacosmetics.com
Products cosmetics, hair care
and styling, nail care, self-
tanning lotion, shower gel,
skin care, soap, sun care
Availability boutiques,
distributors, mail order,
specialty stores

Common Scents
128 Main St.
Port Jefferson, NY 11777
631-473-6370
Products aromatherapy,
bathing supply, fragrance for
men and women, soap
Availability Common Scents
stores, mail order

Conair
1 Cummings Point Rd.
Stamford, CT 06904
203-351-9173
800-7-CONAIR
www.conair.com
Products hair care and
styling, hair color, hair styling
tools, razors
Availability beauty supply
stores, discount department
stores, drugstores, mail order,
supermarkets

**Concept Now
Cosmetics**
12020 Mora Dr., Ste. 9
Santa Fe Springs, CA 90670
502-903-1450
800-CNC-1215
www.conceptnowcosmetics.
com
Products cosmetics, shower
gel, skin care for men and
women
Availability distributors, mail
order

Cosmyl
1 Cosmyl Pl.
Corporate Ridge Industrial
Pk.
Columbus, GA 31907
706-569-6100
800-262-4401
Products cosmetics,
fragrance for women, nail
care, skin care for men and
women, toiletries
Availability boutiques,
department stores, J.C.
Penney stores, Sears stores,
specialty stores

Cot 'N Wash, Inc.
502 The Times Bldg.
Ardmore, PA 19003
610-896-4373
800-355-WASH
www.cotnwash.com
Products fine washables
detergent, household supply
Availability boutiques,
cooperatives, department
stores, health food stores,
mail order, specialty stores
♥

Country Comfort
P.O. Box 2716
Lake Arrowhead, CA 92352
909-337-4667
800-462-6617
Products baby care, healing
salve, lip care
Availability health food
stores, mail order

Country Save
19704 60th Ave. N.E.
Arlington, WA 98223
360-435-9868
www.countrysave.com
Products all-purpose cleaner,
bleach, dish detergent,
laundry detergent
Availability health food
stores, supermarkets
♥

Countryside USA
P.O. Box 38
Conneautville, PA 16406
814-587-6331
800-447-8901
www.countrysidefarm.org
Products aromatherapy,
cinnamon sticks, essential oil,
mulling spices, potpourri,
wardrobe sachets
Availability boutiques,
department stores,
drugstores, mail order
♥

Crabtree & Evelyn, Ltd.
102 Peake Brook Rd.
P.O. Box 167
Woodstock, CT 06281-0167
800-272-2873
www.crabtree-evelyn.com
Products air freshener, baby
care, candles, deodorant,
fragrance for men and
women, hair care, massage
oil/lotion, razors, shaving
supply, shower gel, skin care,
soap
Availability boutiques,
Crabtree & Evelyn stores,
department stores, specialty
stores, Web site

Crown Royale, Ltd.
P.O. Box 5238
99 Broad St.
Phillipsburg, NJ 08865
908-859-6488
800-992-5400
Products carpet cleaner,
companion animal care,
fragrance for men and
women, household supply,
shaving supply, toiletries
Availability distributors, mail
order
♥

Cuccio Naturalé
29120 Ave. Paine
Valencia, CA 91355
800-762-6245
www.starnail.com
Products aromatherapy, nail
care, skin care
Availability beauty supply
stores, salons, spas

COMPANIES THAT
DON'T TEST ON ANIMALS

Dallas Manufacturing Company
4215 McEwen Rd.
Dallas, TX 75244
800-256-8669
www.thebrinkmanncorp.com
Products companion animal care
Availability companion animal supply stores, discount department stores, mail order, supermarkets, wholesale

Damp Rid, Inc.
7701 Southland Blvd.
Ste. 301
Orlando, FL 32809
407-851-6230
888-DAMPRID
www.damprid.com
Products household supply, mold and mildew prevention
Availability discount department stores, Home Depot, mail order, supermarkets

Decleor USA
P.O. Box 1005
Darien, CT 06820-1005
212-838-1771
www.decleor.com
Products aftershave lotion, hypo-allergenic skin care for men and women, lip care, makeup remover, self-tanning lotion, shaving gel, sun care
Availability boutiques, Decleor stores, department stores, skin care salons, spas, specialty stores

Deeply Founded Beauty
16 Garden Gate Ct.
St. Charles, MO 63304
636-936-1963
www.deeplyfoundedbeauty. com
Products aromatherapy, baby care, bathing supply, insect repellent, lip care, nail care, skin care, soap
Availability Web site

Dena Corporation
850 Nichaolas Blvd.
Elk Grove Village, IL 60007
847-593-3041
800-932-3362
www.denacorp.com
Products body care, hair care and styling, hair color, shower gel
Availability drugstores, supermarkets

Denise Chaplin n.y.c.
90 W. Houston St.
New York, NY 10012
212-473-7853
www.denisechaplinnyc.com
Products vegan makeup brushes
Availability Henri Bendel (call 800-HBENDEL to order), Web site

Deodorant Stones of America
9420 E. Doubletree Rd.
Unit 101
Scottsdale, AZ 85258
480-451-4981
800-279-9318
www.deodorantstones.com
Products deodorant, foot care, herbal supplements, toiletries, vitamins
Availability drugstores, health food stores, mail order, supermarkets
♥

Derma-E
4485 Runway St.
Simi Valley, CA 93063
800-521-3342
www.derma-e.com
Products acne treatment, aromatherapy, hair care, hypo-allergenic skin care for men and women, soap
Availability beauty supply stores, health food stores, mail order

Dermalogica
1001 Knox St.
Torrance, CA 90502
310-352-4784
800-345-2761
www.dermalogica.com
Products cosmetics, deodorant, hair care, hypo-allergenic skin care for men and women, lip care, self-tanning lotion, shaving cream, shower gel, sun care
Availability boutiques, physicians, skin care salons, spas, specialty stores

Dermatologic Cosmetic Laboratories
20 Commerce St.
East Haven, CT 06512
203-467-1570
800-552-5060
Products acne treatment, bathing supply, dandruff shampoo, hair care, makeup remover, nail care, skin care for men and women, soap, sun care
Availability aestheticians, physicians

Desert Essence
27460 Ave. Scott
Valencia, CA 91355-3473
800-645-5768
www.desertessence.com
Products acne treatment,
aromatherapy, baby bathing
supply, body care, dental
floss, hair care, lip care,
massage oil/lotion,
mouthwash, skin care,
soap, toothpaste
Availability boutiques, health
food stores, specialty stores

DeSoto
900 E. Washington St.
P.O. Box 609
Joliet, IL 60433
815-727-4931
Products household supply
Availability drugstores,
supermarkets

Devita Natural Skin Care
6845 W. McKnight Loop
Ste. A
Glendale, AZ 85308
602-547-9174
877-2-DEVITA
www.devita.net
Products lip care, skin care,
sun care
Availability drugstores, health
food stores, mail order, Web
site

Diamond Brands
1800 Cloquet Ave.
Cloquet, MN 55720
800-777-7942
www.diamondbrand.com
Products cosmetics, nail care
Availability discount
department stores,
drugstores, supermarkets

Dickinson Brands, Inc.
31 E. High St.
P.O. Box 149
East Hampton, CT 06424
860-267-2279
888-860-2279
www.witchhazel.com
Products skin care, soap
Availability drugstores, health
food stores, mail order

Dirty Kitty Vegan Soapworks
501 Park Ave.
Elyria, OH 44035
440-452-3763
www.cleanvegan.com
Products body care, foot
care, lip care, soap
Availability gift stores, health
food stores, mail order,
supermarkets, Web site
♥

Donna Karan
767 Fifth Ave.
New York, NY 10153
212-572-4200
www.donnakaran.com
Products fragrance for men
and women
Availability department
stores

Dr. A.C. Daniels, Inc.
109 Worcester Rd.
Webster, MA 01570
508-943-5563
800-547-3760
www.drdaniels.com
Products companion animal
shampoo and vitamins
Availability companion
animal supply stores, mail
order, Web site

Dr. Bronner's Magic Soaps
P.O. Box 28
Escondido, CA 92033-0028
760-743-2211
www.drbronner.com
Products all-purpose cleaner,
baby care, castile soaps
Availability drugstores, health
food stores, mail order,
supermarkets
♥ 🛒

Dr. Goodpet
P.O. Box 4547
Inglewood, CA 90309
310-672-3269
800-222-9932
www.goodpet.com
Products companion animal
care: homeopathics,
shampoo, vitamins
Availability companion
animal supply stores,
drugstores, health food
stores, mail order, Web site

Dr. Hauschka Skin Care
59C North St.
Hatfield, MA 01038
413-247-9907
800-247-9907
www.drhauschka.com
Products body care, bathing
supply, cosmetics, deodorant,
hair care, herbal
supplements, lip care,
massage oil, nail care, shower
gel, skin care for men and
women, sun care
Availability boutiques, health
food stores, specialty stores

Dr. Ken's (Floss & Go)
1112 Montana Ave., Ste. D
Santa Monica, CA 90403
310-394-6700
877-FLOSSGO
www.drkens.net
Products breath freshener,
dental floss, dental gum,
mouthwash, toothpaste,
Availability drugstores, health
food stores, supermarkets
♥

**Dr. Singha's Natural
Therapeutics**
2500 Side Cove
Austin, TX 78704
512-444-2862
800-856-2862
www.drsingha.com
Products air freshener,
aromatherapy, bathing supply,
massage oil/lotion,
nonprescription therapy
Availability boutiques, health
food stores, mail order, spas,
specialty stores
♥

Earth Friendly Products
44 Green Bay Rd.
Winnetka, IL 60093
www.ecos.com
Products air freshener, all-
purpose cleaner, automatic
dishwashing detergent,
bathroom cleaner, bleach,
companion animal care,
cream cleanser, dish
detergent, drain cleaner, fruit
and vegetable wash, furniture
polish, glass cleaner, laundry
detergent, paper products,
stain and odor remover,
starch, toilet cleaner
Availability distributors,
health food stores, mail
order
♥

Earth Mama Angel Baby
3959 S.W. Halcyon Rd.
Tualatin, OR 97062
503-638-0487
www.earthmamaangelbaby.com
Products aromatherapy, baby
bathing supply, baby care,
body care, lip care, massage
oil, personal care, pregnancy
care
Availability health food
stores, supermarkets, Web
site
♥

Earthly Matters
(First Coast Industrial)
2950 St. Augustine Rd.
Jacksonville, FL 32207
904-398-1458
800-398-7503
Products air freshener, carpet
cleaner, furniture polish,
household supply, laundry
detergent
Availability distributors,
health food stores, mail
order
♥

Earth's Beauty
663 Hopi Tr.
Dewey, AZ 86327
928-772-0119
888-586-9719
www.earthsbeauty.com
Products aromatherapy,
cosmetics, fragrance for
women
Availability mail order, salons,
Web site

Earth Science
P.O. Box 40339
Santa Barbara, CA 93140
805-684-4525
800-347-5211
www.earthessentials.com
Products acne treatment,
aftershave lotion, deodorant,
hair care, hypo-allergenic
skin care for men and
women, makeup remover,
shaving cream
Availability cooperatives,
health food stores, mail
order

Earth Solutions
1123 Zonolite Rd., #8
Atlanta, GA 30306
404-347-9900
800-883-3376
www.earthsolutions.com
Products air freshener;
aromatherapy; bubble bath;
candles; car care; hypo-
allergenic skin care for men,
women, and children
Availability boutiques,
cooperatives, health food
stores, independent sales
representatives, mail order,
specialty stores, Web site
♥

Earth 2 Jane
389 Fifth Ave., Ste. 1100
New York, NY 10016
212-779-0544
www.townleygirl.com
Products cosmetics
Availability discount
department stores,
drugstores, supermarkets

Eberhard Faber (Sanford)
2711 Washington Blvd.
Bellwood, IL 60104
708-547-5525
800-438-3703
www.sanfordcorp.com
Products ink, office supply,
writing instruments
Availability department
stores, drugstores, mail order,
office supply stores,
supermarkets

E. Burnham Cosmetics
7117 N. Austin Ave.
Niles, IL 60714
847-647-2121
Products hair care, hypo-
allergenic skin care for men
and women
Availability drugstores, health
food stores, mail order

Ecco Bella Botanicals
1123 Rte. 23
Wayne, NJ 07470
973-696-7766
www.eccobella.com
Products air freshener,
aromatherapy, bathing supply,
cosmetics, dandruff
shampoo, fragrance for
women, hair care, hypo-
allergenic skin care, makeup
remover, shower gel, soap,
vegan makeup brushes
Availability boutiques,
drugstores, health food
stores, mail order, specialty
stores

Eco-DenT International
P.O. Box 325
Twin Lakes, WI 53181
262-889-8561
888-ECO-DENT
www.eco-dent.com
Products dental floss, dental
gum, mouthwash,
toothbrushes, toothpowders
Availability cooperatives,
dentists, drugstores, health
food stores, mail order,
supermarkets

Eco Design Company
1330 Rufina Cir.
Santa Fe, NM 87507
505-438-3448
800-621-2591
www.bioshieldpaint.com
Products automatic
dishwashing detergent, dish
detergent, floor cleaner, floor
finish, glass cleaner, liquid
soap, paint, soap, toilet
cleaner, wood-finishing supply
Availability environmentally
friendly stores, mail order

Eco Lips, Inc.
329 10th Ave. S.E.
Cedar Rapids, IA 52401
866-326-5477
319-364-2477
www.ecolips.com
Products lip care
Availability drugstores, health
food stores, sporting-goods
stores, supermarkets, Web
site

Ecover
2340 S. Eastern Ave.
Los Angeles, CA 90040
323-720-5730
800-449-4925
www.ecover.com
Products all-purpose cleaner,
automatic dishwashing
detergent, bleach, cream
cleanser, dish detergent,
fabric softener, fine
washables detergent, laundry
detergent, soap, stain
remover
Availability cooperatives,
health food stores, mail
order, supermarkets

**Edward & Sons Trading
Company**
P.O. Box 1326
Carpinteria, CA 93014
805-684-8500
www.edwardandsons.com
Products hair care,
household supply
Availability boutiques,
cooperatives, health food
stores, mail order, specialty
stores

COMPANIES THAT
DON'T TEST ON ANIMALS

Elizabeth Grady Face First
222 Boston Ave.
Medford, MA 02155
800-FACIALS
www.elizabethgrady.com
Products cosmetics, hypo-
allergenic skin care for men
and women, makeup
remover, sun care
Availability boutiques,
distributors, Elizabeth Grady
Face First stores, mail order,
specialty stores

Elizabeth Van Buren Aromatherapy
P.O. Box 7542
303 Potrero St., #33 & #7
Santa Cruz, CA 95061
800-710-7759
www.evb-aromatherapy.com
Products aromatherapy, body
care, essential oils, hypo-
allergenic skin care for
women, insect repellant,
massage oil, soap
Availability department
stores, drugstores, health
food stores, mail order,
massage therapists
♥

Ella Baché
8 W. 36th St., 8th Fl.
New York, NY 10018
212-279-9411
800-922-2430
www.ellabache.com
Products after-sun care, body
care, depilatory, makeup
remover, self-tanning lotion,
skin care, soap, sun care
Availability department
stores, drugstores, Ella Baché
store, health food stores,
mail order, salons, spas, Web
site

ELON Nail & Skin Essentials
38 Church Ave.
Wareham, MA 02571
508-295-2200
800-414-ELON
www.ilovemynails.com
Products hair care, nail care,
skin care
Availability dermatologists,
mail order, salons, spas, Web
site

Eminence Organic Skin Care
2001-1715 Cook St.
Vancouver, BC V5Y 3T6
Canada
www.eminenceorganics.com
604-602-4787
888-747-6342
Products skin care
Availability salons, spas
♥

English Ideas, Ltd.
3111 W. Alpine
Santa Ana, CA 92704
714-436-1120
800-547-5278
www.liplast.com
Products cosmetics, lip care,
nonprescription therapy,
personal care, skin care, sun
care
Availability beauty supply
stores, department stores,
salons

EO Products
15 A Koch Rd.
Madera, CA 94925
415-945-1900
800-570-3775
www.eoproducts.com
Products all-purpose cleaner,
aromatherapy, bath salts,
body care, bubble bath, dish
detergent, foot care, hair
care, lip care, shower gel, skin
care, soap
Availability department
stores, natural food stores

Essence of Vali, Inc.
179 Christopher St.
New York, NY 10014
212-242-0576
www.essenceofvali.com
Products aromatherapy, bath
oil, fragrance for women,
massage oil
Availability drugstores, health
food stores, spas, Web site

The Essential Oil Company
8225 S.E. Seventh Ave.
Portland, OR 97202-6428
503-872-8735
800-729-5912
www.essentialoil.com
Products aromatherapy,
fragrance for men and
women, hair care, insect
repellent, soap, soap-making
supply, sun care
Availability cooperatives,
health food stores, mail
order, Web site

Essential 3
145 Hummingbird Ln.
Talent, OR 97540
541-535-1866
888-48-AROMA
www.essentialthree.com
Products essential oils
Availability cooperatives,
health food stores, mail
order, spas, Web site

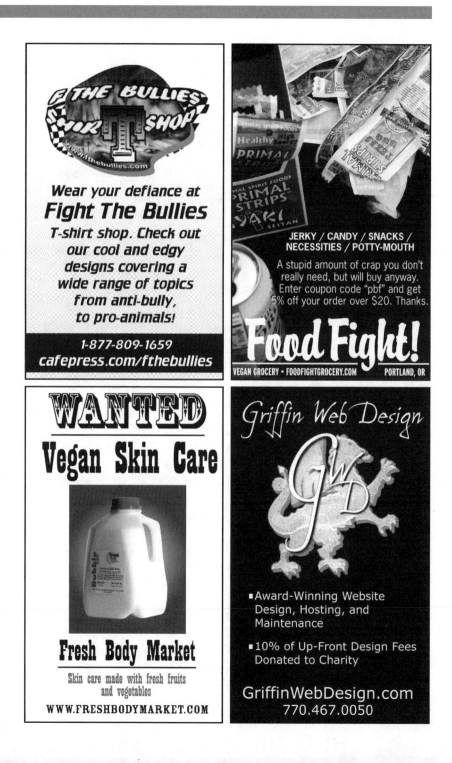

COMPANIES THAT
DON'T TEST ON ANIMALS

Estée Lauder
767 Fifth Ave.
New York, NY 10153
212-572-4200
www.esteelauder.com
Products bathing supply,
cosmetics, deodorant,
fragrance for men and
women, lip care, nail care,
self-tanning lotion, shaving
supply, skin care, soap, sun
care
Availability department
stores, specialty stores

Eucerin (Beiersdorf)
BDF Plaza
360 Martin Luther King Dr.
Norwalk, CT 06856-5529
203-853-8008
www.beiersdorf.com
Products skin care, sun care
Availability drugstores,
supermarkets

European Gold
33 S.E. 11th St.
Grand Rapids, MN 55744
218-326-0266
800-946-5395
Products hypo-allergenic skin
care for men and women,
sun care
Availability health clubs,
salons, tanning salons

Every Body, Ltd.
1738 Pearl St., Ste. 107F
Boulder, CO 80302
303-440-0188
800-748-5675
www.everybodyltd.com
Products aromatherapy, body
care, bubble bath, dental
hygiene, deodorant,
fragrance for men and
women, hair care, lip care,
massage oil, shaving cream,
shower gel, skin care, soap,
sun care
Availability Every Body Ltd.
stores, mail order, Web site

Exuberance
International Inc.
270 Albert St., 12th Fl.
Ottawa, Ontario K1P 5G8
Canada
877-671-2639
www.exuberance.ca
Products bathing supply,
body care, foot care, lip care,
massage oil, salt scrubs, skin
care
Availability drugstores, health
food stores, yoga studios

FACE Atelier
P.O. Box 556, 7620 Elbow Dr.
Calgary, AB T2V 1K2
Canada
403-301-3391
www.faceatelier.com
Products cosmetics
Availability Web site

The Face Food Shoppe
21298 Pleasant Hill Rd.
Boonville, MO 65233
816-882-6858
800-882-6858
Products acne treatment,
aromatherapy, bathing supply,
hypo-allergenic skin care for
men and women, soap,
toiletries
Availability cooperatives,
The Face Food Shoppe
store, health food stores,
independent sales
representatives, mail order

Faith Products, Ltd.
Unit 2, The Saw Mill, East St.
Bury, Lancashire BL9 0RU
England
011 44 16 1764 2555
www.faithproducts.com
Products bubble bath, hair
care, massage oil, skin care
for men and women, shower
gel, soap
Availability health food
stores, mail order

Farmavita USA
(Chuckles)
P.O. Box 5126
Manchester, NH 03109
603-669-4228
800-221-3496
www.sukesha.com
Products hair color
Availability salons

Faultless Starch/Bon
Ami
510 Walnut St.
Kansas City, MO 64106-1209
816-842-1230
www.bonami.com
Products air freshener, all-
purpose cleaner, copper and
stainless-steel cleaner, glass
cleaner, laundry detergent,
powdered cleanser, starch,
wrinkle remover
Availability drugstores,
supermarkets

Fernand Aubry
22, Rue de Canmartin
75009 Paris
France
011 33 149 84 24 00
Products cosmetics,
fragrance for men and
women, nail care, self-tanning
lotion, skin care for men and
women, sunburn relief, sun
care, toiletries
Availability boutiques,
department stores, salons,
spas, specialty stores

Fish Hair Styling
304 Park Ave. S., 11th Fl.
New York, NY 10010
212-590-2471
www.shave.com
Products hair care and
styling
Availability salons, spas,
specialty stores, Web site

Fleabusters/Rx for Fleas
6555 N.W. Ninth Ave.
Ste. 412
Ft. Lauderdale, FL 33309
954-351-9244
800-666-3532
www.fleabuster.com
Products companion animal
shampoo, insect repellent
Availability cooperatives,
independent sales
representatives, mail order,
veterinarians

Flirt!
767 Fifth Ave.
New York, NY 10153
866-887-8884
www.flirtcosmetics.com
Products cosmetics
Availability Kohl's
department stores, Web site

**Flower Essences of Fox
Mountain**
P.O. Box 381
Worthington, MA 01098
www.foxmountain.net
Products nonprescription
therapy, vibrational medicine
Availability bookstores,
health food stores, mail
order, supermarkets
♥

Food Lion
P.O. Box 1330
Salisbury, NC 28145-1330
704-633-8250
www.foodlion.com
Products baby care, hair
care, household supply, nail
care, office supplies, razors,
skin care, toiletries, vitamins
Availability Food Lion stores

Forest Essentials
601 Del Norte Blvd., Ste. F
Channel Islands, CA 93030
805-278-8975
800-301-7767
www.forestessentials.com
Products body care, hair
care, shower gel, skin care,
soap
Availability beauty supply
stores, department stores,
environmentally friendly
stores, gift shops, mail order

Forest Nymphs
2287 Euclid Ave.
Long Beach, CA 90815
562-331-9506
www.forestnymphs.com
Products aromatherapy, body
care, candles
Availability boutiques, Web
site

**Forever Living Products
International**
7501 E. McCormick Pkwy.
Scottsdale, AZ 85258
480-998-8888
888-440-2563
www.foreverliving.com
Products aftershave lotion,
all-purpose cleaner, bathing
supply, companion animal
shampoo, cosmetics,
deodorant, hair care and
styling, herbal supplements,
lip care, self-tanning lotion,
shaving supply, skin care,
soap, sun care, toothpaste,
vitamins
Availability independent sales
representatives, mail order

Forever New Company
156 St. Regis Crescent S.
North York, ON M3J 1Y8
Canada
416-630-3295
800-463-CARE
www.fashionessentials.com
Products fine washables
detergent
Availability department
stores, drugstores, mail order,
supermarkets, Web site
♥

**Forever New
International**
4701 N. Fourth Ave.
Sioux Falls, SD 57104-0403
605-331-2910
800-977-0004
www.forevernew.com
Products fine washables
detergent, stain remover
Availability boutiques,
department stores,
drugstores, mail order,
specialty stores
♥

Framesi USA
400 Chess St.
Coraopolis, PA 15108
412-269-2950
800-321-9648
Products hair care, hair color,
permanent waves
Availability salons

COMPANIES THAT
DON'T TEST ON ANIMALS

Frank T. Ross
(Nature Clean)
6550 Lawrence Ave. E.
Scarborough, ON M1C 4A7
Canada
416-282-1107
www.franktross.com
Products all-purpose cleaner,
automatic dishwashing
detergent, bathroom cleaner,
bleach, carpet cleaner, dish
detergent, fabric softener,
fine washables detergent,
fruit and vegetable wash,
glass cleaner, glue, hair care,
laundry detergent, oven
cleaner, soap, stain remover,
toilet cleaner
Availability cooperatives,
department stores,
drugstores, health food
stores, mail order,
supermarkets
♥

Freeda Vitamins
36 E. 41st St.
New York, NY 10017
212-685-4980
800-777-3737
www.freedavitamins.com
Products herbal
supplements, vitamins
Availability cooperatives,
drugstores, health food
stores, mail order,
supermarkets

Freeman Beauty
10474 Santa Monica Blvd.
Ste. 300
Los Angeles, CA 90025
310-446-9300
www.freemanbeauty.com
Products body care, bubble
bath, foot care, hair care,
shower gel, skin care
Availability drugstores, mass
merchandisers,
supermarkets, Web site
♥

French Transit
398 Beach Rd.
Burlingame, CA 94010
650-548-9600
800-829-7625
www.thecrystal.com
Products deodorant, hair
care, hypo-allergenic skin
care
Availability boutiques,
department stores,
drugstores, health food
stores, mail order, specialty
stores, Web site
♥

Fresh Body Market
2030 Century Center Blvd.
Ste. H
Irving, TX 75062
214-441-1861
866-313-7374
www.freshbodymarket.com
Products bathing supply,
body care, soap
Availability department
stores, mail order, Web site
♥ 🛒

**Frontier Natural
Products Co-op**
3021 78th St., Box 299
Norway, IA 52318
319-227-7996
800-669-3275
www.frontiercoop.com
Products aromatherapy,
bathing supply, fragrance for
women, herbal supplements,
household supply, soap,
toiletries, vitamins
Availability cooperatives,
health food stores, mail
order
♥

Fruit of the Earth
P.O. Box 152044
Irving, TX 75015-2044
972-790-0808
800-527-7731
www.fote.com
Products bathing supply,
bubble bath, hair care, herbal
supplements, holistic health
care, self-tanning lotion, skin
care, sunburn relief, sun care
Availability discount
department stores,
drugstores, supermarkets

Gabriel Cosmetics, Inc.
P.O. Box 50130
Bellevue, WA 98015
425-688-8663
800-497-6419
www.gabrielcosmeticsinc.
com
Products aromatherapy, baby
care, cosmetics, hair care, lip
care, skin care, sun care
Availability Gabriel
Cosmetics store, health
food stores, mail order,
supermarkets
♥

Garden Botanika
11121 Willows Rd. N.E.
Ste. 210
Redmond, WA 98052-1016
800-968-7842
www.gardenbotanika.com
Products bubble bath,
cosmetics, deodorant,
fragrance for women, hair
care, nail care, shower gel,
skin care for men and
women, soap
Availability mail order, Web
site
🛒

The Garmon Corporation
27461-B Diez Rd.
Temecula, CA 92590
909-296-6308
888-628-8783
www.naturvet.com
Products companion animal shampoo and vitamins
Availability companion animal supply stores, mail order

Georgette Klinger
501 Madison Ave.
New York, NY 10022
212-244-0250
800-KLINGER
www.georgetteklinger.com
Products acne treatment, body care, lip care, makeup remover, skin care
Availability Georgette Klinger salons, mail order, specialty stores

Gigi Laboratories
2220 Gaspar Ave.
Los Angeles, CA 90040
213-728-2999
www.aiibeauty.com
Products body care, depilatory, skin care
Availability beauty supply stores, boutiques, specialty stores

Giovanni Cosmetics
21580 S. Wilmington Ave.
Carson, CA 90810
310-952-9960
800-563-5468
www.giovannicosmetics.com
Products hair care
Availability boutiques, cooperatives, drugstores, health food stores, mail order, specialty stores, supermarkets

Glad Rags
P.O. Box 12648
Portland, OR 97212
503-282-0436
800-799-4523
www.gladrags.com
Products feminine hygiene, soap, vitamins
Availability distributors, health-care practitioners, health food stores, mail order, Web site, wholesale

Golden Pride/Rawleigh
1501 Northpoint Pkwy.
Ste. 100
West Palm Beach, FL 33407
561-640-5700
www.rawleigh.com
Products all-purpose cleaner, herbal supplements, laundry detergent, skin care, toilet cleaner, vitamins, water filtration
Availability independent sales representatives, mail order

Goldwell USA
581 Corporate Blvd.
Linthicum Heights, MD 21090
800-288-9118
www.goldwellusa.com
Products hair care and styling, hair color
Availability salons

good skin
767 Fifth Ave.
New York, NY 10153
866-352-8338
www.goodskindermcare.com
Products skin care
Availability Kohl's department stores, Web site

göt2b
1063 McGaw, Ste. 100
Irvine, CA 92614
949-794-5500
www.citreshine.com
Products hair care and styling
Availability beauty supply stores, drugstores, supermarkets

■

Great American, The Wholefood Farmacy
117 E. Main St.
Rogersville, TN 37857
423-921-7848
866-550-8638
www.thewholefoodfarmacy.com
Products bathing supply, body care, essential oils, hair care, holistic health care, lip care, skin care, soap, toothpaste
Availability The Wholefood Farmacy store, Web site
♥ 🛒

Green Ban
P.O. Box 146
Norway, IA 52318
319-446-7495
www.greenban.com
Products companion animal care, insect-bite treatment, insect repellent
Availability cooperatives, health food stores, mail order, specialty stores, sporting goods stores
♥

Green Girl Basics
46 W. Tulane Rd.
Columbus, OH 43202
614-263-3938
www.greengirlbasics.com
Products body care, soap,
soap-making supply
Availability health food
stores, mail order, specialty
stores, Web site

Greenridge Herbals
9237 S. Mica Mine Rd.
Littleton, CO 80127
866-250-4372
www.greenridgeherbals.com
Products aromatherapy,
bubble bath, candles, lip care,
skin care
Availability health food
stores, mail order, Web site
♥

Gustavo Cosmetics
1200 N. Veitch St., Ste. 812
Arlington, VA 22201
703-908-9620
800-58-FACE1
www.gustavocosmetics.com
Products aromatherapy,
cosmetics, hypo-allergenic
skin care, shower gel, soap,
sun care
Availability boutiques,
Gustavo Cosmetics stores,
mail order, salons, specialty
stores

Halo, Purely for Pets
3438 E. Lake Rd., #14
Palm Harbor, FL 34685
727-937-3376
800-426-4256
www.halopets.com
Products companion animal
shampoo and vitamins, insect
repellent
Availability companion animal
supply stores, health food
stores, mail order, Web site

Hard Candy
729 Farad St.
Costa Mesa, CA 92627
949-515-1250
866-330-CANDY
www.hardcandy.com
Products bathing supply, body
care, cosmetics, fragrance for
women, hair styling, lip care,
nail care
Availability boutiques,
department stores, Web site

Hawaiian Resources
68-309 Crozier Dr.
Waialua, HI 96791
808-636-2300
www.mailorderhawaii.com
Products bathing supply,
soap, sun care
Availability boutiques,
drugstores, health food
stores, mail order, specialty
stores, supermarkets, Web
site
♥

The Health Catalog
460 Oak St., Ste. 104
Glendale, CA 91204
800-651-0062
www.healthcatalog.com
Products herbal
supplements, vitamins
Availability health food
stores, mail order

Healthy Times
13200 Kirkham Way
Ste. 104
Poway, CA 92064
858-513-1550
www.healthytimes.com
Products baby care, organic
and vegan baby food
Availability baby stores,
cooperatives, health food
stores, mail order
♥

Heather's Natural &
Organic Cleaning
Products
3515 Eastham
Culver City, CA 90232
877-JASON-01
www.heathersnaturals.com
Products air freshener, all-
purpose cleaner, bathroom
cleaner, glass cleaner,
powdered cleanser
Availability health food
stores, mail order
♥

Hello Kitty
389 Fifth Ave., Ste. 1100
New York, NY 10016
212-779-0544
www.townleygirl.com
Products cosmetics, lip care,
nail care
Availability discount
department stores,
drugstores, supermarkets

The Hempery
4713 Stillbrook
Houston, TX 77035
614-662-4367
800-BUY-HEMP
www.hempery.com
Products hair care, herbal
supplements, massage oil,
skin care
Availability health food
stores, mail order

Henri Bendel
712 Fifth Ave.
New York, NY 10019
212-247-1100
800-HBENDEL
www.henribendel.com
Products fragrance for
women
Availability Henri Bendel
stores, mail order

Herbal Logix
1063 McGaw, Ste. 100
Irvine, CA 92614
949-794-5500
www.citreshine.com
Products hair care
Availability beauty supply
stores, drugstores,
supermarkets

**Herbal Products &
Development**
P.O. Box 1084
Aptos, CA 95001
831-688-8706
www.centralcoastnutrition.
com
Products nutritional
supplements, skin care,
vitamins
Availability health food
stores, mail order, Web site

Hobé Laboratories, Inc.
6479 S. Ash Ave.
Tempe, AZ 85283
480-413-1950
800-528-4482
www.hobelabs.com
Products body care, hair care
and styling, hair loss
treatment, hand sanitizers,
pain relief, psoriasis
treatment, skin care for men
and women, weight loss aids
Availability boutiques,
cooperatives, department
stores, drugstores, health
food stores, mail order,
specialty stores,
supermarkets, Web Site

Hoke2
1147 Fewtrell Dr.
Campbell, CA 95008
408-559-9200
877-438-4652
www.hoke2.com
Products razors, shaving
cream
Availability department
stores, health food stores,
mail order

**Home Service Products
Company**
P.O. Box 129
Lambertville, NJ 08530
609-397-8674
Products fine washables
detergent, laundry detergent
Availability mail order
♥

House of Cheriss
2374 Traymore Rd.
University Heights, OH
44118
216-397-0036
Products body care, massage
lotion, skin care for men and
women
Availability health food
and specialty stores, mail
order

H2O Plus
845 W. Madison
Chicago, IL 60607
312-850-9283
800-242-BATH
www.h2oplus.com
Products acne treatment,
bubble bath, candles,
fragrance for men and
women, hair care, lip care,
shaving cream, shower gel,
skin care for men and
women, sun care
Availability boutiques,
department stores, duty-free
shops, H2O Plus stores, mail
order, specialty stores

Huish Detergents
3540 W. 1987 S.
P.O. Box 25057
Salt Lake City, UT 84125
801-975-3100
800-776-6702
www.huish.com
Products automatic
dishwashing detergent,
bleach, dish detergent, fabric
softener, glass cleaner, hand
sanitizer, household supply,
laundry detergent, rinse aid,
stain remover, water softener
Availability department
stores, discount department
stores, drugstores,
supermarkets

Ida Grae
(Nature's Colors Cosmetics)
424 La Verne Ave.
Mill Valley, CA 94941
415-388-6101
Products cosmetics, hypo-
allergenic skin care for men
and women
Availability boutiques,
cooperatives, health food
stores, mail order, specialty
stores

Il-Makiage
107 E. 60th St.
New York, NY 10022
800-722-1011
Products cosmetics, hair
care, hair color, hypo-
allergenic skin care for
women, nail care
Availability boutiques,
cooperatives, health spas, Il-
Makiage stores, mail order,
salons, specialty stores

ILONA
3201 E. Second Ave.
Denver, CO 80206-5203
303-322-3000
888-38-ILONA
www.ilona.com
Products bathing supply,
cosmetics, fragrance for men
and women, hair care, lip
care, nail care, self-tanning
lotion, shaving supply, skin
care for men and women,
soap, sun care, theatrical
makeup
Availability boutiques,
department stores, ILONA
stores, mail order, specialty
stores, Web site

Innovative Formulations
1810 S. Sixth Ave.
S. Tucson, AZ 85713
520-628-1553
800-487-9510
www.innovativeformulations.
com
Products paint
Availability mail order
♥

Internal Health
www.internalhealth.com
Products vitamins
Availability health food
stores, Web site

IQ Products Company
16212 State Hwy. 249
Houston, TX 77086
281-444-6454
www.iqproducts.com
Products car care, glass
cleaner, hair care, insect
repellent, nail care, shaving
supply, sun care
Availability discount
department stores,
drugstores, supermarkets

**Iredale Minderal
Cosmetics, Ltd.**
28 Church St.
Great Barrington, MA 01230
413-644-9900
www.janeiredale.com
Products cosmetics
Availability dermatologists,
salons, spas

Jacki's Magic Lotion
145 Hummingbird Ln.
Talent, OR 97540
800-355-8428
www.jackismagiclotion.com
Products body care, massage
lotion
Availability cooperatives,
health food stores, mail
order, spas, Web site

James Austin Company
P.O. Box 827
115 Downieville Rd.
Mars, PA 16046
724-625-1535
800-245-1942
www.jamesaustin.com
Products all-purpose cleaner,
ammonia, bleach, carpet
cleaner, dish detergent, fabric
softener, glass cleaner,
laundry detergent, oven
cleaner, soap
Availability discount
department stores,
drugstores, supermarkets

Jane
767 Fifth Ave.
New York, NY 10153
212-572-4200
www.janecosmetics.com
Products cosmetics, nail care
Availability department
stores, drugstores

**Jason Natural
Cosmetics**
8468 Warner Dr.
Culver City, CA 90232-2484
310-838-7543
800-JASON-05
www.jason-natural.com
Products aftershave lotion,
aromatherapy, dandruff
shampoo, dental floss,
deodorant, hair care and
styling, hypo-allergenic skin
care, massage oil,
mouthwash, shaving cream,
shower gel, soap, sun care,
toothpaste
Availability cooperatives,
health food stores, mail
order, Web site

**Jeanne Rose
Aromatherapy**
219 Carl St.
San Francisco, CA 94117-
3804
415-564-6785
www.jeannerose.net
Products aromatherapy,
companion animal care,
herbal supplements, hypo-
allergenic skin care for men
and women, toiletries
Availability boutiques,
cooperatives, health food
stores, independent sales
representatives, mail order,
specialty stores

Jess' Bee Natural Products
P.O. Box 82512
Columbus, OH 43202
614-784-8565
www.beenaturallipbalm.com
Products body care, lip care
Availability drugstores, health food stores, mail order, specialty stores, Web site

Jessica McClintock
1400 16th St.
San Francisco, CA 94103-5181
415-553-8200
www.jessicamcclintock.com
Products fragrance for women
Availability department stores, Jessica McClintock boutiques, mail order

Jheri Redding (Conair)
1 Cummings Point Rd.
Stamford, CT 06902
203-351-9000
800-7-CONAIR
www.conair.com
Products hair care, hair styling tools, permanent waves, toiletries
Availability beauty supply stores, discount department stores, drugstores, supermarkets

Joe Blasco Cosmetics
6107 Metrowest Blvd., #101
Orlando, FL 32835
323-671-1088
800-634-0008
www.joeblasco.com
Products bathing supply, cosmetics, skin care, theatrical makeup
Availability beauty supply stores, boutiques, mail order, salons, spas, specialty stores

John Amico Expressive Hair Care Products
4731 W. 136th St.
Crestwood, IL 60445
708-824-4000
800-676-5264
www.johnamico.com
Products dandruff shampoo, ethnic personal care, hair care and styling, hair color, herbal supplements, permanent waves, self-tanning lotion, shower gel, skin care
Availability mail order, salons

John Masters Organics
77 Sullivan St.
New York, NY 10012
212-343-9590
800-599-2450
www.johnmasters.com
Products body care, companion animal shampoo, dandruff shampoo, hair care, lip care, shower gel, skin care
Availability department stores, health food stores, John Masters Organics store, mail order, salons, spas, Web site

John Paul Mitchell Systems
9701 Wilshire Blvd.
Ste. 1205
Beverly Hills, CA 90212
310-248-3888
800-321-JPMS
www.paulmitchell.com
Products hair care and styling, hair color, shaving cream, skin care, soap
Availability salons

JOICO Laboratories
P.O. Box 42308
Los Angeles, CA 90042-0308
626-968-6111
800-44-JOICO
www.joico.com
Products hair care and styling, hair color, permanent waves
Availability salons

■

Jolen Creme Bleach
25 Walls Dr.
P.O. Box 458
Fairfield, CT 06824
203-259-8779
Products bleaching cream
Availability discount department stores, drugstores, supermarkets

Jo Malone
767 Fifth Ave.
New York, NY 10153
866-305-4706
www.jomalone.com
Products acne treatment, bathing supply, body care, candles, fragrance for women, hair care, skin care
Availability department stores, Web site

Joyful Hands Holistic Pet Care and Bakery
613 Laguna Ave.
El Cajon, CA 92020
619-440-4409
www.joyfulhands.com
Products companion animal health care, organic vegan treats, supplements
Availability mail order, specialty companion animal supply stores, Web site

COMPANIES THAT
DON'T TEST ON ANIMALS

J.R. Liggett, Ltd.
R.R. 2, Box 911
Cornish, NH 03745
603-675-2055
www.jrliggett.com
Products dandruff shampoo,
hair care
Availability boutiques,
cooperatives, drugstores,
health food stores,
independent sales
representatives, mail order,
specialty stores
♥

Juice Beauty, Inc.
38 Miller Ave., #180
Mill Valley, CA 94941
707-573-1966
888-90-JUICE
www.juicebeauty.com
Products skin care
Availability boutiques, mail
order, specialty stores, Web
site

Jurlique
2714 Apple Valley Rd. N.E.
Atlanta, GA 30319-3139
800-854-1110
www.jurlique.com
Products aftershave lotion,
aromatherapy, baby bathing
supply, bubble bath,
cosmetics, deodorant,
fragrance for women, hair
care, massage oil, nail care,
shaving gel, skin care, soap
Availability mail order, salons,
spas

Kate Spade Beauty
454 Broome St.
New York, NY 10013
800-519-3778
www.katespade.com
Products fragrance for
women, shower gel, skin
care, soap
Availability Kate Spade stores

Katonah Scentral
51 Katonah Ave.
Katonah, NY 10536
914-232-7519
Products aromatherapy, baby
care, dental hygiene, essential
oil, fragrance for men and
women, hair care, hair color,
shaving supply, toiletries,
toothbrushes
Availability Katonah Scentral
stores, mail order

Kenic Pet Products
400 Lincoln St.
Lawrenceburg, KY 40342-
1282
800-228-7387
www.glo-marr-kenic.com
Products companion animal
care
Availability companion
animal supply stores,
drugstores, grooming shops,
hardware stores, health food
stores, independent sales
representatives, mail order,
veterinarians

Kenra
6501 Julian Ave.
Indianapolis, IN 46219
317-356-6491
800-428-8073
www.kenra.com
Products dandruff shampoo,
ethnic personal care, hair
care and styling
Availability salons

Kiehl's
109 Third Ave.
New York, NY 10003
212-677-3171
800-KIEHLS1
www.kiehls.com
Products acne treatment,
aftershave lotion, baby
bathing supply, companion
animal shampoo, cosmetics,
equine care, fragrance for
men and women, hair care
and styling, lip care, shaving
cream, skin care, sun care
Availability department
stores, Kiehl's stores, mail
order
■

King of Shaves
304 Park Ave. S., 11th Fl.
New York, NY 10010
212-590-2471
www.shave.com
Products shaving supply, skin
care
Availability drugstores, heath
food stores, mail order,
supermarkets, Web site

Kirk's Natural Products

7329 W. Harrison St.
Forest Park, IL 60130
708-771-5475
800-825-4757
www.kirksnatural.com
Products acne treatment,
baby bathing supply, body
care, castile soap, hair care,
massage oil, skin care, soap
Availability drugstores, heath
food stores, mail order,
supermarkets, Web site
♥

Kiss My Face

P.O. Box 224
144 Main St.
Gardiner, NY 12525
845-255-0884
800-262-KISS
www.kissmyface.com
Products air freshener,
aromatherapy, baby care,
bubble bath, candles,
deodorant, hair care, insect
repellant, lip care,
mouthwash, shaving cream,
shower gel, skin care for
men and women, soap, sun
care, toothpaste
Availability boutiques,
cooperatives, drugstores,
health food stores, mail
order, massage therapists,
salons, Web site
🐇

KMS Research

4712 Mountain Lakes Blvd.
Redding, CA 96003
530-244-6000
800-DIAL-KMS
www.kmshaircare.com
Products dandruff shampoo,
hair care and styling,
permanent waves
Availability salons
■

KSA Jojoba

19025 Parthenia St., #200
Dept. PE
Northridge, CA 91324
818-701-1534
www.jojoba-ksa.com
Products acne treatment,
body care, companion
animal shampoo, foot care,
fragrance for women, hair
care, lip care, skin care, soap
Availability mail order
♥

LaCrista

801 N. East St.
Frederick, MD 21701
301-682-9611
www.lacrista.com
Products aromatherapy,
candles, hypo-allergenic skin
care for men and women,
soap
Availability health food
stores, mail order, specialty
stores, Web site
♥

Lady of the Lake

P.O. Box 6969
Brookings, OR 97415-0355
541-469-3354
www.shopladyofthelake.com
Products aromatherapy,
holistic health care, vitamins,
water filtration
Availability health food
stores, independent sales
representatives, mail order
♥

Lakon Herbals

R.R. 1, Box 4710
J.R. Liggett, Ltd.
Montpelier, VT 05602
802-223-5563
800-865-2566
www.lakonherbals.com
Products aromatherapy, body
care, insect repellent, lip care,
massage oil
Availability health food
stores, mail order
♥

Lamas Beauty

6222 Wilshire Blvd., Ste. 302
Los Angeles, CA 90048
323-936-1281
877-604-6521
www.lamasbeauty.com
Products bathing supply,
body care, color cosmetics,
dandruff shampoo, hair care
and styling, skin care
Availability health food
stores, mail order, Web site
♥

La Mer

767 Fifth Ave.
New York, NY 10153
866-850-9400
www.cremedelamer.com
Products body care, skin
care
Availability department
stores, Web site

LaNatura

5033 Exposition Blvd.
Los Angeles, CA 90016
323-766-0060
800-352-6288
www.lanatura.com
Products baby bathing
supply, bubble bath, candles,
shower gel, skin care, soap
Availability boutiques, health
food stores, LaNatura stores,
mail order, specialty stores
♥

COMPANIES THAT
DON'T TEST ON ANIMALS

Lander Company, Inc.
2000 Lenox Dr., Ste. 202
Lawrenceville, NJ 08648
609-219-0930
800-4-LANDER
www.lander-hbc.com
Products baby bathing
supply, bubble bath,
companion animal shampoo,
dandruff shampoo, dental
hygiene, deodorant, ethnic
personal care, hair care,
shaving supply, shower gel,
soap, sun care
Availability discount
department stores,
drugstores, supermarkets

L'anza Research
International
429 Santa Monica Blvd.
Ste. 510
Santa Monica, CA 90401
310-393-5227
www.lanza.com
Products dandruff shampoo,
hair care and styling, hair
color
Availability salons

La Prairie
680 Fifth Ave.
New York, NY 10019
212-506-0840
800-821-5718
www.laprairie.com
Products cosmetics,
fragrance for men and
women, makeup remover,
skin care for men and
women, sun care
Availability boutiques,
department stores, specialty
stores

Lather
76 N. Fair Oaks Ave.
Pasadena, CA 91103
626-397-9050
800-6-LATHER
www.lather.com
Products aromatherapy, hair
care, lip care, shaving cream,
shower gel, skin care, soap
Availability department
stores, Lather stores, mail
order, Web site

Lauren Amoresse
International
4981 Irwindale Ave.
Bldg. 15, Ste. 600
Irwindale, CA 91706
800-258-7931
www.amoresse.com
Products hand sanitizer,
jewelry cleaner, nail care, nail
polish remover
Availability salons

Lee Pharmaceuticals
1434 Santa Anita Ave.
S. El Monte, CA 91733
800-950-5337
www.leepharmaceuticals.com
Products aftershave lotion,
depilatory, hair care, lip care,
mouthwash, nail care,
nonprescription therapy,
toothbrushes, toothpaste,
vitamins
Availability boutiques,
drugstores, supermarkets

Liberty Natural
Products
8120 S.E. Stock St.
Portland, OR 97215-2346
503-256-1227
800-289-8427
www.libertynatural.com
Products air freshener,
aromatherapy, baby care,
body care, dental hygiene,
deodorant, fragrance for
women, hair care, massage
oil, nonprescription therapy,
soap, toothbrushes, vitamins
Availability boutiques,
cooperatives, discount
department stores,
drugstores, health food
stores, specialty stores,
supermarkets

Life in the Woods
408 Peel St.
Whitby, ON L1N 3Y4
Canada
905-668-9898
www.lifeinthewoods.ca
Products soap
Availability boutiques,
department stores, drug-
stores, health food stores,
spas, supermarkets
♥

Life Tree Products
P.O. Box 40339
Santa Barbara, CA 93140
805-684-4525
800-347-5211
www.goturtle.com
Products all-purpose cleaner,
aromatherapy, automatic
dishwashing detergent,
bathing supply, bathroom
cleaner, body care, dish
detergent, laundry detergent,
massage lotion, soap,
toiletries
Availability cooperatives,
drugstores, health food
stores, mail order,
supermarkets
♥

COMPANIES THAT
DON'T TEST ON ANIMALS

Lily of Colorado
P.O. Box 437
Henderson, CO 80640
303-455-4194
800-333-LILY
www.lilyofcolorado.com
Products lip care, massage
oil, skin care
Availability health food
stores, mail order

Lime-O-Sol Company
(The Works)
P.O. Box 395
Ashley, IN 46705
219-587-9151
800-448-5281
www.limeosol.com
Products bathroom cleaner,
drain cleaner, glass cleaner,
toilet cleaner
Availability department
stores, discount department
stores, drugstores,
supermarkets

Lip-Ink International
105 Eucalyptus Dr.
El Segundo, CA 90245
310-414-9246
www.lipink.com
Products air freshener,
aromatherapy, cosmetics,
deodorant, fragrance for
women, hair care, hair color,
makeup remover, skin care
Availability salons, spas, Web
site
♥

**Little Forest Natural
Baby Products**
501 Union St., Ste. 201
Nashville, TN 37219
615-986-0138
888-329-BABY
www.littleforest.com
Products baby care
Availability baby boutiques,
health food stores,
independent sales
representatives, mail order
♥

Liz Claiborne Cosmetics
1441 Broadway
New York, NY 10018
212-354-4900
www.lizclaiborne.com
Products bathing supply,
deodorant, fragrance for
men and women, shaving
supply, soap, toiletries
Availability department
stores, Liz Claiborne stores

Lobob Laboratories
1440 Atteberry Ln.
San Jose, CA 95131-1410
408-432-0580
800-83-LOBOB
www.loboblabs.com
Products contact lens
cleaner and solution
Availability discount
department stores,
drugstores, mail order,
supermarkets
♥

Logona USA
554-E Riverside Dr.
Asheville, NC 28801
704-252-1420
800-648-6654
www.logona.de/E/
Products baby care, body
care, cosmetics, dandruff
shampoo, deodorant,
fragrance for men, hair care,
hair color, hypo-allergenic
skin care for men and
women, makeup remover,
massage oil, shaving cream,
shower gel, soap, sun care,
toiletries, toothpaste
Availability boutiques,
cooperatives, health food
stores, mail order, specialty
stores

**Lotus Moon Natural
Skin Care**
1271 Washington Ave., #720
San Leandro, CA 94577
501-638-6819
888-762-2667
www.lotusmoonbiz.com
Products acne treatment,
aromatherapy, bathing supply,
body care, hair care, psoriasis
treatment, rosacea
treatment, skin care
Availability health food
stores, supermarkets, Web
site

Louise Bianco Skin Care
13655 Chandler Blvd.
Sherman Oaks, CA 91401
818-786-2700
800-782-3067
www.louisebianco.com
Products deodorant, hypo-
allergenic skin care for men
and women, lip care, self-
tanning lotion, shower gel,
sun care
Availability mail order, salons,
Web site

M.A.C. Cosmetics
100 Alden Rd.
Markham, ON L3R 4C1
Canada
905-470-7877
800-588-0070
www.maccosmetics.com
Products cosmetics, ethnic
personal care, fragrance for
women, hypo-allergenic skin
care for men and women,
nail care, theatrical makeup
Availability department
stores, M.A.C. Cosmetics
stores

Magick Botanicals
3412 W. MacArthur Blvd., #K
Santa Ana, CA 92704
714-957-0674
800-237-0674
www.magickbotanicals.com
Products acne treatment, all-
purpose cleaner, automatic
dishwashing detergent, baby
bathing supply, hair care and
styling, laundry detergent,
skin care for men and
women, soap
Availability health food
stores, mail order
♥

The Magic of Aloe
7300 N. Crescent Blvd.
Pennsauken, NJ 08110
856-662-3334
800-257-7770
www.magicofaloe.com
Products bathing supply,
cosmetics, hair care, shaving
supply, skin care for men and
women, soap, sun care,
toiletries, vitamins
Availability independent sales
representatives, mail order,
salons, Web site

Malibu Sun Products
1014 Laurel St., Ste. 200
Brainerd, MN 56401-3779
218-829-6238
800-421-7314
Products after-sun care, self-
tanning lotion, sun care
Availability tanning salons
♥

Mallory Pet Supplies
740 Rinkin Rd. N.E.
Albuquerque, NM 87107
505-836-4033
800-824-4464
www.mallorypet.com
Products companion animal
shampoo
Availability companion
animal supply stores, mail
order

Marcal Paper Mills
1 Market St.
Elmwood Park, NJ 07407
201-796-4000
www.marcalpaper.com
Products paper products
Availability drugstores,
supermarkets
♥

**Marché Image
Corporation**
P.O. Box 1010
Bronxville, NY 10708
800-753-9980
Products hypo-allergenic skin
care
Availability independent sales
representatives, mail order

**Marie-Véronique Skin
Therapy**
2826 A Kelsey St.
Berkeley, CA 94705
www.m-vskintherapy.com
Products body care, hypo-
allergenic skin care, sun care
Availability drugstores, salons,
Web site

Marilyn Miglin Institute
112 E. Oak St.
Chicago, IL 60611
312-943-1120
800-662-1120
www.marilynmiglin.com
Products candles, cosmetics,
fragrance for men and
women, makeup remover,
skin care, sun care, vitamins
Availability independent sales
representatives, mail order,
Marilyn Miglin Institute

Mary Kay
16251 N. Dallas Pkwy.
P.O. Box 779045
Dallas, TX 75379-9045
972-687-6300
800-MARYKAY
www.marykay.com
Products bathing supply,
cosmetics, fragrance for
women, nail care, shower gel,
skin care, soap, sun care
Availability independent sales
representatives, Web site

Masada
P.O. Box 4118
Chatsworth, CA 91313
818-717-8300
800-368-8811
www.masada-spa.com
Products bath salts, body
care, foot care, shower gel
Availability cooperatives,
health food stores, mail
order
♥

COMPANIES THAT
DON'T TEST ON ANIMALS

Mastey de Paris
25413 Rye Canyon Rd.
Valencia, CA 91355
661-257-4814
800-6-MASTEY
www.mastey.com
Products fragrance for men
and women, hair care and
styling, hair color, permanent
waves, skin care, sun care
Availability mail order, salons

Meadow View Garden
P.O. Box 407
Wyoming, RI 02898
800-499-7037
www.meadowviewimports.
com
Products skin care, toiletries
Availability health food
stores
♥

Mehron
100 Red Schoolhouse Rd.
Chestnut Ridge, NY 10977
914-426-1700
800-332-9955
www.mehron.com
Products cosmetics,
theatrical makeup
Availability boutiques,
costume/novelty stores, mail
order, party supply stores,
specialty stores

Mère Cie
3840 Finley Ave., Bldg. 37
Ste. D
Santa Rosa, CA 95407
707-528-7597
800-832-4544
www.merecie.com
Products aromatherapy,
fragrance for men and
women
Availability boutiques, health
food stores, independent
sales representatives, mail
order, specialty stores, Web
site
♥

Merle Norman
9130 Bellanca Ave.
Los Angeles, CA 90045
310-641-3000
www.merlenorman.com
Products cosmetics,
deodorant, fragrance for
men and women, lip care,
nail care, skin care, soap
Availability Merle Norman
salons

Merry Hempsters
P.O. Box 1301
Eugene, OR 97440
541-345-9317
888-SEED-OIL
www.merryhempsters.com
Products body care, lip care,
massage oil
Availability drugstores, health
food stores, specialty stores,
supermarkets, Web site

Method Products, Inc.
30 Hotaling Pl., 3rd Fl.
San Francisco, CA 94111
415-931-2695
866-9-METHOD
www.methodhome.com
Products air freshener, all-
purpose cleaner, bathroom
cleaner, candles, cleaning
wipes, dish detergent, floor
cleaner, furniture polish, glass
cleaner, liquid soap, shower
cleaner, stainless-steel cleaner
Availability health food
stores, Target, Web site

Mia Rose Products, Inc.
177-F Riverside Ave.
Newport Beach, CA 92663
714-662-5465
800-292-6339
www.miarose.com
Products air freshener,
all-purpose cleaner,
aromatherapy, stain remover
Availability boutiques,
cooperatives, distributors,
drugstores, health food
stores, mail order,
specialty stores,
supermarkets, Web site
♥

Michelle Lazár
International
1299 E. San Bernardino Ave.
San Bernardino, CA 92408-
2943
909-796-3100
Products skin care
Availability health food
stores, mail order

Micro Balanced
Products
225 Country Rd.
Tenafly, NJ 07670
800-626-7888
Products deodorant, hypo-
allergenic skin care for men
and women, sun care,
toiletries
Availability health food
stores, mail order
♥

Mill Creek Botanicals
879 W. 190th St.
Gardena, CA 90248
702-651-6116
866-447-6758
www.millcreekbotanicals.com
Products dandruff shampoo,
deodorant, hair care and
styling, hair loss, shower gel,
skin care, soap
Availability drugstores, health
food stores, supermarkets

Mira Linder Spa in the City
29935 Northwestern Hwy.
Southfield, MI 48034
800-321-8860
www.miralinder.net
Products hypo-allergenic skin
care for men and women,
sun care
Availability mail order, Mira
Linder Spa in the City stores

Montagne Jeunesse
P.O. Box 39-F
Denver, CO 80239-0019
800-552-5742
www.montagnejeunesseusa.com
Products aromatherapy,
bathing supply, body care,
depilatory, foot care, hair
care, lip care, shower gel, skin
care, soap, toiletries
Availability boutiques,
cooperatives, department
stores, discount department
stores, drugstores, health
food stores, independent
sales representatives,
specialty stores,
supermarkets

■

Moonshine Soap
542 Luther Palmer Rd.
Cleveland, GA 30528
706-219-2404
www.moonshinesoap.com
Products soap
Availability boutiques, mail
order, salons, spas, Web site

Morrocco Method
135 Howard Ave.
Los Osos, CA 93402-2322
805-534-1600
www.morroccomethod.com
Products body care, dandruff
shampoo, hair care and
styling, hair color
Availability health food
stores, Web site

Mother's Little Miracle
27520 Hawthorne Blvd.
Ste. 125
Rolling Hills Estate, CA
90274
310-544-7125
Products air freshener, baby
care, stain and odor remover
Availability boutiques,
discount department stores,
distributors, drugstores, mail
order, specialty stores
♥

Mountain Green
12650 N. 103rd Pl.
Scottsdale, AZ 85260
www.mtngreen.com
480-922-0817
866-686-4733
Products dish detergent,
glass cleaner, laundry
detergent
Availability health food
stores, specialty stores,
supermarkets
♥

Mountain Ocean, Ltd.
5150 Valmont Rd.
Boulder, CO 80301
303-444-2781
www.mountainocean.com
Products hair care, lip care,
pregnancy care, skin care,
soap, sun care
Availability health food
stores, mail order,
supermarkets, Web site

Mr. Christal's
10877 Wilshire Blvd.
12th Fl.
Los Angeles, CA 90024
310-824-2508
800-426-0108
www.mrchristals.com
Products companion animal
shampoo, fruit and vegetable
wash
Availability mail order

Murad, Inc.
2121 Rosecrans Ave., 5th Fl.
El Segundo, CA 90245
310-726-3344
888-99-MURAD
www.murad.com
Products acne treatment,
dandruff shampoo, hair care,
hypo-allergenic skin care, sun
care, vitamins
Availability beauty supply
stores, mail order, Murad
stores, salons, spas, specialty
stores

Mystic Wonders, Inc.
15872 Ivy Ave.
Breda, IA 51436-8609
712-775-2050
888-452-4968
www.mysticwondersinc.com
Products all-purpose cleaner,
laundry balls, toilet cleaner,
water treatment
Availability health food
stores, mail order
♥

Naava, Inc.
4971 Pernod Ave., Ste. A
St. Louis, MO 63139-1251
314-832-3544
Products aromatherapy, lip
care, skin care, soap
Availability health food
stores, online, mail order
♥

Nadina's Cremes
3813 Middletown Branch
Rd.
Vienna, MD 21869
410-901-1052
800-722-4292
www.nadinascremes.com
Products body care, candles,
soap
Availability boutiques,
cooperatives, drugstores,
environmentally friendly
stores, health food stores,
independent sales
representatives, mail order,
specialty stores

Naikid, Inc.
P.O. Box 435
Union, NJ 07083
www.naikid.com
Products bathing supply, soap
Availability Web site

Nala Barry Labs
5312 Derry Ave., #P
Agoura, CA 91301
818-597-1447
www.nalabarry.com
Products companion animal
shampoo and supplements
Availability boutiques,
companion animal supply
stores, cooperatives, health
food stores, specialty stores
♥

**Narwhale of High Tor,
Ltd.**
591 S. Mountain Rd.
New City, NY 10956
914-634-8832
800-MD-CREAM
www.mdcream.com
Products acne treatment,
cosmetics, hypo-allergenic
skin care for men and
women, scar cream, sun care
Availability mail order,
physicians, skin care clinics

Natracare
14901 E. Hampden Ave.
Ste. 190
Aurora, CO 80014
www.natracare.com
Products baby bathing
supply, feminine hygiene
Availability cooperatives,
drugstores, health food
stores, mail order,
supermarkets, Web site
♥

Naturade
14370 Myford Rd., Ste. 100
Irvine, CA 92602
714-573-4800
800-367-2880
www.naturade.com
Products body care; bubble
bath; dandruff shampoo; hair
care; herbal supplements;
holistic health care; hypo-
allergenic skin care for men
and women; nutritional
shakes, supplements, bars;
shower gel; soap; toiletries;
vitamins
Availability boutiques,
cooperatives, health food
stores, mail order, specialty
stores, supermarkets

Natura Essentials
2845 Harriet Ave. S.
Minneapolis, MN 55406
888-606-0055
www.naturaessentials.com
Products air freshener,
aromatherapy, candles,
essential oil, fragrance for
men and women, skin care
for men and women
Availability boutiques,
distributors, health food
stores, mail order, spas,
specialty stores

**Natural Animal Health
Products**
7000 U.S. 1 N.
St. Augustine, FL 32095
904-824-5884
800-274-7387
www.naturalanimal.com
Products companion animal
vitamins, insect repellent
Availability companion
animal supply stores,
cooperatives, health food
stores, veterinarians

Natural Bodycare
100 S. Lucia Ave., #2
Redondo Beach, CA 90277
310-323-2125
www.natural-bodycare.com
Products aftershave lotion,
aromatherapy, baby bathing
supply, bath salts, body care,
dandruff shampoo, ethnic
personal care, fragrance for
men and women, hair care,
household supply, lip care,
makeup remover, massage
oil, psoriasis treatment,
shower gel, skin care,
sunburn relief, sun care,
toiletries
Availability health food
stores, mail order

COMPANIES THAT
DON'T TEST ON ANIMALS

Natural Chemistry
76 Progress Dr.
Stamford, CT 06902
203-316-4479
800-753-1233
www.naturalchemistry.com
Products companion animal
shampoo, pool supply, stain
remover
Availability cooperatives,
environmentally friendly
stores, health food stores,
mail order

Naturally Yours, Alex
1848 Murray Ave.
Clearwater, FL 33755
727-443-7479
NYAshampoo@aol.com
Products companion animal
care
Availability companion
animal supply stores, e-mail
(10% of e-mail orders will
be donated to PETA), health
food stores, holistic
veterinarians, mail order
♥

Natural Research People
810 Dean Creek
Lavina, MT 59046
406-575-4343
Products companion animal
care
Availability companion animal
supply stores, cooperatives,
health food stores, mail
order, veterinarians
♥

Natural Salt Lamps
6448 W. Francisco
Chicago, IL 60645
312-224-2710
www.natural-salt-lamps.com
Products bath salts, body
care, body scrubs, skin care
Availability mail order, Web
site
♥

Nature Clean
(Frank T. Ross & Sons, Ltd.)
6550 Lawrence Ave. E.
Scarborough, ON M1C 4A7
Canada
416-282-1107
www.franktross.com
Products all-purpose cleaner,
automatic dishwashing
detergent, bathroom cleaner,
bleach, carpet cleaner, dish
detergent, fabric softener, fine
washables detergent, fruit and
vegetable wash, glass cleaner,
glue, hair care, laundry
detergent, oven cleaner, soap,
stain remover, toilet cleaner
Availability cooperatives,
department stores,
drugstores, health food
stores, mail order,
supermarkets
♥

Nature's Acres
8984 E. Weinke Rd.
North Freedom, WI 53951
608-522-4492
800-499-HERB
www.naturesacres-herbals.
com
Products aromatherapy, baby
care, bath salts, body oils,
companion animal care,
fragrance for men and
women, herbal supplements,
lip care, shaving supply, skin
care for men and women,
soap, vitamins
Availability boutiques, health
food stores, mail order,
specialty stores

Nature's Best
(Natural Research People)
810 Dean Creek
Lavina, MT 59046
406-575-4343
Products companion animal
care
Availability companion
animal supply stores, health
food stores, mail order
♥

Nature's Country Pet
1765 Garnet Ave., Ste. 12
San Diego, CA 92109
619-230-1058
Products companion animal
care
Availability companion
animal supply stores, health
food stores, mail order
♥

Nature's Gate
9200 Mason Ave.
Chatsworth, CA 91311
818-882-2951
800-327-2012
www.naturesgatebeauty.com
Products bubble bath, dental
floss, deodorant, hair care,
hypo-allergenic skin care for
women, lip care, shaving
cream, soap, sun care,
toothpaste
Availability discount
department stores, health
food stores, mail order,
supermarkets

Nature's Plus
548 Broadhollow Rd.
Melville, NY 11747-3708
631-293-0030
800-645-9500
www.naturesplus.com
Products herbal
supplements, vitamins
Availability health food
stores

Nature's Soap Dish
5913 N.E. 102nd Ave.
Ste. I
Vancouver, WA 98662
360-885-4727
www.naturessoapdish.com
Products baby care, bathing supply, cosmetics, fragrance for women, hair care, lip care, skin care, soap, sun care
Availability boutiques, mail order, Nature's Soap Dish store, Web site

Naturopathica
74 Montauk Hwy.
East Hampton, NY 11937
631-329-8792
800-669-7618
www.naturopathica.com
Products aromatherapy, bath oil and salts, body care, body oil, foot care, massage oil, skin care for women and men, shaving supply, shower gel, soap
Availability mail order, Naturopathica stores, spas, supermarkets, Web site

Neo Soma
P.O. Box 393
Deerfield, IL 60015
847-607-0677
877-NEO-SOMA
www.neosoma.com
Products hair care, skin care
Availability country clubs, health clubs, pro shops, sporting goods stores
♥

New Age Products
P.O. Box 1153
Port Townsend, WA 98368
800-736-0612
Products all-purpose cleaner
Availability cooperatives, health food stores
♥

Neways
150 E. 400 N.
Salem, UT 84653
801-423-2800
800-998-7233
www.neways.com
Products air freshener, all-purpose cleaner, aromatherapy, baby bathing supply, bubble bath, cosmetics, deodorant, dish detergent, hair care and styling, hypo-allergenic skin care for men and women, laundry detergent, massage oil, mouthwash, nail care, shaving cream, sun care, toothpaste, vitamins
Availability boutiques, distributors, mail order, specialty stores

New Chapter Extracts
P.O. Box 1947
Brattleboro, VT 05302
802-257-0018
800-543-7279
www.new-chapter.com
Products hair care, herbal extracts, nonprescription therapy, skin care, vitamins
Availability aestheticians, cooperatives, health food stores, mail order, physicians
♥

New Vision International
8322 E. Hartford Dr.
Scottsdale, AZ 85255
800-MINERALS
www.newvision.com
Products aromatherapy, bathing supply, hair care, herbal supplements, nonprescription therapy, shower gel, skin care, vitamins
Availability distributors
♥

Nexxus Products
P.O. Box 1274
Santa Barbara, CA 93116
805-968-6900
www.nexxusproducts.com
Products dandruff shampoo, hair care and styling, hair color, permanent waves
Availability salons

Nikken
52 Discovery Rd.
Irvine, CA 92618
949-789-2000
800-669-8859
www.nikken.com
Products nutritional supplements
Availability specialty stores

Nirvana
P.O. Box 325
Twin Lakes, WI 53181
262-889-8501
800-824-6396
Products aromatherapy, incense
Availability cooperatives, drugstores, health food stores, mail order
♥

Nivea (Beiersdorf)
BDF Plaza
360 Martin Luther King Dr.
Norwalk, CT 06856-5529
203-854-8000
www.nivea.com
Products aftershave lotion, body care, shaving cream, shower gel, skin care for women and men
Availability drugstores, supermarkets

No Common Scents
Kings Yard
220 Xenia Ave.
Yellow Springs, OH 45387
937-767-4261
800-686-0012
www.nocommonscents.com
Products aromatherapy, bath
crystals, herbal supplements,
incense, massage oil
Availability mail order, No
Common Scents store

Nordstrom Cosmetics
865 Market St.
San Francisco, CA 94103
800-7-BEAUTY
www.nordstrom.com
Products acne treatment,
candles, cosmetics, massage
oil, skin care
Availability mail order,
Nordstrom department
stores

Norelco
1010 Washington Blvd.
P.O. Box 120015
Stamford, CT 06912-0015
203-973-0200
www.norelco.com
Products electric razors
Availability department
stores, drugstores,
supermarkets

North American
Naturals
55 Pittsfield Rd.
Lenox, MA 01240
877-833-SOAP
www.nansoap.com
Products soap
Availability drugstores, health
food stores, mail order, Web
site
♥

North Country
Glycerine Soap
7888 County Rd., #6
Maple Plain, MN 55359-
9552
612-479-3381
800-667-1202
www.specialtysoapsinternatio
nal.com
Products companion animal
shampoo, hair care, hypo- ·
allergenic skin care, insect
repellent, soap
Availability boutiques,
companion animal supply
stores, cooperatives,
department stores,
drugstores, health food
stores, mail order, specialty
stores, sports supply stores

N/R Laboratories, Inc.
868 Pleasant Valley Dr.
Springboro, OH 45066
800-223-9348
937-433-9570
www.norinse.com
Products bathing supply, hair
care
Availability distributors, mail
order

Nu Skin International
1 NuSkin Plz.
75 W. Center
Provo, UT 84601
800-487-1000
www.nuskin.com
Products acne treatment,
baby care, cosmetics, dental
floss, deodorant, fragrance
for men and women, hair
care and styling, lip care,
mouthwash, skin care for
men and women, sun care,
toothbrushes, toothpaste
Availability distributors, mail
order, Web site

NutriBiotic
P.O. Box 238
Lakeport, CA 95453
800-225-4345
www.nutribiotic.com
Products bubble bath,
deodorant, mouthwash,
nonprescription therapy, self-
tanning lotion, shower gel,
skin care, vitamins
Availability health food
stores, Web site

Nutri-Cell
1038 N. Tustin, Ste. 309
Orange, CA 92867-5958
714-953-8307
Products herbal
supplements, lip care, skin
care, vitamins
Availability health food
stores, mail order
♥

Nutri-Metics
International
5333 Westheimer, Ste. 820
Houston, TX 77056
713-589-5150
www.myavalla.com
Products aftershave lotion,
all-purpose cleaner,
aromatherapy, body care,
cosmetics, deodorant,
footcare, fragrance for men
and women, hair care,
household supply, laundry
detergent, massage oil, self-
tanning lotion, shaving supply,
shower gel, skin care,
sunburn relief, sun care,
toiletries
Availability distributors, mail
order

NuTru, Inc.
627 11th St.
Wilmette, IL 60091
847-251-0513
www.nutru.com
Products vitamins
Availability drugstores, health
food stores, mail order, Web
site
♥

Oliva, Ltd.
P.O. Box 4387
Reading, PA 19606
610-779-7854
Products soap
Availability health food
stores, mail order
♥

**ONLY YOURx Skin
Care**
25028 Kearny Ave.
Valencia, CA 91355
800-877-4849
www.onlyyourx.com
Products acne treatment,
cosmetics, skin care for men
and women, sun care
Availability day spas,
physicians, professional skin
care salons and clinics

OPI Products
13034 Saticoy St.
N. Hollywood, CA 91605
818-759-2400
800-341-9999
www.opi.com
Products cosmetics, lip care,
nail care, sun care
Availability beauty supply
stores, salons

Orange-Mate
P.O. Box 883
Waldport, OR 97394
541-563-3290
800-626-8685
www.orangemate.com
Products air freshener,
all-purpose cleaner, fabric
freshener, glass cleaner
Availability cooperatives,
department stores, discount
department stores,
drugstores, health food
stores, independent sales
representatives, mail order,
specialty stores
♥

**Organic Health and
Beauty**
12400 Ventura Blvd., #123
Studio City, CA 91604
866-787-3642
www.organichealthandbeauty
.com
Products body care, hair
care, skin care, vitamins
Availability health food
stores, mail order, Web site
♥

**The Organic Make-Up
Company, Inc.**
11 Crawford St.
Markham, ON L6C 2L4
Canada
905-479-9295
www.organicmakeup.ca
Products cosmetics, body
care, lip care, skin care
Availability mail order, Web
site

Organix South
6290-B 147th Ave. N.
Clearwater, FL 33760
727-531-8801
888-989-6336
www.organixsouth.com
Products baby care, bathing
supply, body care, companion
animal care, dental hygiene,
hair care, insect repellent, nail
care, skin care, soap
Availability health food
stores, mail order

Oriflame USA
P.O. Box 977
Waxhaw, NC 28173
704-843-3102
www.oriflame.com
Products bubble bath,
cosmetics, deodorant,
fragrance for men and
women, hair care, hypo-
allergenic skin care for men
and women, shower gel
Availability distributors, mail
order

**Origins Natural
Resources**
767 Fifth Ave.
New York, NY 10153
212-572-4100
www.origins.com
Products aromatherapy, baby
bathing supply, bubble bath,
cosmetics, deodorant, ethnic
personal care, fragrance for
women, hair care and styling
products, lip care, self-tanning
lotion, shaving cream, skin
care, soap, sun care, vegan
makeup brushes
Availability boutiques,
department stores, Origins
stores, specialty stores

Orjene Natural Cosmetics
3352 81st St., #22
Jackson Heights, NY 11372-1338
718-937-2666
800-886-7536
Products cosmetics, hair care, shaving supply, skin care for men and women, sun care, toiletries
Availability cooperatives, health food stores, mail order

Orlane, Inc.
555 Madison Ave.
New York, NY 10022
212-750-1111
800-535-3628
www.orlaneusa.com
Products cosmetics, fragrance for women, hypo-allergenic skin care for women, nail care, sun care
Availability boutiques, department stores, specialty stores

Orly International
9309 Deering Ave.
Chatsworth, CA 91311
818-998-1111
800-275-1111
www.orlyproducts.com
Products nail care
Availability discount department stores, drugstores

Osea International
30765 Pacific Coast Hwy.
Ste. 205
Malibu, CA 90265
310-589-1942
800-576-6732
www.oseaskin.com
Products bathing supply, body care, lip care, makeup remover, massage oil, skin care
Availability spas, specialty stores, Web site
♥

Otto Basics—Beauty 2 Go!
P.O. Box 9023
Rancho Santa Fe, CA 92067
800-598-OTTO
Products cosmetics
Availability department stores, mail order

Oxyfresh Worldwide
1301 N. Lakewood Dr.
Coeur D Alene, ID 83814-4912
800-223-7374
www.oxyfreshww.com
Products air freshener, all-purpose cleaner, bathing supply, companion animal shampoo, hair care, herbal supplements, laundry detergent, mouthwash, skin care for men and women, soap, toothbrushes, toothpaste
Availability independent sales representatives, mail order
♥

Parlux Fragrances
3725 S.W. 30th Ave.
Ft. Lauderdale, FL 33312
954-316-9008
800-727-5895
www.parlux.com
Products deodorant, fragrance for men and women, shower gel, sun care
Availability boutiques, department stores, drugstores, specialty stores
♥

Pathmark Stores
200 Milik St.
Carteret, NJ 07008
732-499-3000
www.pathmark.com
Products air freshener, baking soda, dental hygiene, razors, toothbrushes, vitamins
Availability Pathmark supermarkets and drugstores

Patricia Allison Natural Beauty Products
4470 Monahan Rd.
La Mesa, CA 91941
619-444-4163
800-858-8742
Products bathing supply, cosmetics, fragrance for women, hair care, hypo-allergenic skin care for men and women, lip care, sun care, toiletries
Availability mail order

Paul Mazzotta
P.O. Box 96
Reading, PA 19607
610-376-2250
www.ecocare.com
Products bathing supply,
body care, cosmetics,
dandruff shampoo, hair care
and styling, hair color, hypo-
allergenic skin care for men
and women, lip care,
massage oil, nail care,
permanent waves, sun care,
toiletries
Availability mail order, Paul
Mazzotta stores, salons
♥

Paul Mitchell
9701 Wilshire Blvd.
Ste. 1205
Beverly Hills, CA 90212
800-321-JPMS
www.paulmitchell.com
Products hair care and
styling, hair color, shaving
cream, skin care,
sun care
Availability salons

Paul Penders
303 Industri Keda
07000 Kuah
LangKawi
www.paulpenders.com
604-966-9688
Products body care,
cosmetics, hair care, hypo-
allergenic skin care, makeup
remover
Availability department
stores, health food stores,
mail order, Web site

Pet Guard
165 Industrial Loop S.
Unit 5
Orange Park, FL 32073
904-264-8500
800-874-3221
www.petguard.com
Products companion animal
shampoo and vitamins
Availability companion
animal supply stores,
cooperatives,
environmentally friendly
stores, health food stores,
veterinarians

Pets 'N People
(Nature's Miracle)
27520 Hawthorne Blvd.
Ste. 125
Rolling Hills Estate, CA
90274
310-544-7125
Products carpet cleaner,
cleaning supply, litter
treatment
Availability companion
animal supply stores, mail
order ·
♥

Pharmacopia
1525 E. Francisco Blvd., #9
San Rafael, CA 94901
415-455-0112
877-389-9898
www.pharmacopia.net
Products aromatherapy, bath
salts, body care, candles,
massage oil, shower gel, soap
Availability department
stores, drugstores, health
food stores, mail order,
Pharmacopia store, Web site
♥

Pharmagel International
P.O. Box 2288
Monterey, CA 93942
831-649-2300
800-882-4889
Products air freshener, body
oil, breath freshener,
deodorant, fragrance for
women, hypo-allergenic skin
care for men and women, lip
care
Availability boutiques, health
food stores, mail order,
salons, specialty stores
♥

PH Beauty Labs
10474 Santa Monica Blvd.
Ste. 300
Los Angeles, CA 90025
310-446-9300
www.phbeauty.com
Products bathing supply, body
care, foot care, hair care and
styling, skin care
Availability drugstores, mail
order, supermarkets, Web
site
♥

Physicians Formula
1055 W. Eighth St.
Azusa, CA 91702
626-334-3395
www.physiciansformula.com
Products cosmetics, hypo-
allergenic skin care, sun care
Availability drugstores

**Pilot Corporation of
America**
60 Commerce Dr.
Trumbull, CT 06611
203-377-8800
www.pilotpen.com
Products office supply, writing
instruments
Availability catalogs,
drugstores, office supply
stores, supermarkets
♥

COMPANIES THAT
DON'T TEST ON ANIMALS

Pittstown Soapworks
436 Pittstown Rd.
Pittstown, NJ 08867
908-730-8631
Products candles, soap
Availability Pittstown
Soapworks store, mail order
♥

Planet
P.O. Box 48184
Victoria, BC V8Z 7H6
Canada
800-858-8449
www.planetinc.com
Products all-purpose cleaner,
dish detergent, fine
washables detergent, laundry
detergent
Availability cooperatives,
health food stores, mail
order, supermarkets
♥

PlantEssence Natural
Body Care
1631 N.E. Broadway St.
#235
Portland, OR 97232
503-281-9371
800-752-6898
www.plantessence.com
Products air freshener, body
oil, breath freshener,
fragrance for men and
women, lip care, skin care for
men and women, toiletries
Availability boutiques,
cooperatives, health food
stores, mail order, specialty
stores

Power Puff Girls
389 Fifth Ave., Ste. 1100
New York, NY 10016
212-779-0544
www.townleygirl.com
Products cosmetics
Availability discount
department stores,
drugstores, supermarkets

prawduct
1107 Fair Oaks Ave., #334
South Pasadena, CA 90065
323-221-6779
www.thekitchenbeautician.com
Products hair care and
styling
Availability beauty supply
stores, boutiques, drugstores,
mail order, Web site

Prescriptives
767 Fifth Ave.
New York, NY 10153
212-572-4400
Products acne treatment,
bathing supply, cosmetics,
ethnic personal care,
fragrance for women, skin
care, soap, sun care, toiletries
Availability department
stores, specialty stores

Prestige Cosmetics
1601 Green Rd.
Pompano Beach, FL 33064
954-480-9202
800-722-7488
www.prestigecosmetics.com
Products cosmetics, ethnic
personal care
Availability beauty supply
stores, department stores,
drugstores, specialty stores

Prestige Fragrances,
Ltd. (Revlon)
625 Madison Ave.
New York, NY 10022
212-572-5000
Products fragrance for
women
Availability department
stores

The Principal Secret
3340 Ocean Park Blvd.
Ste. 3055
Santa Monica, CA 90405
310-581-6250
800-545-5595
www.principalsecret.com
Products cosmetics, skin care
for men and women
Availability home shopping
networks, JCPenney, mail
order

Professional Pet
Products
1873 N.W. 97th Ave.
Miami, FL 33172
305-592-1992
800-CALL-PPP
Products companion animal
care
Availability companion
animal supply stores,
cooperatives, drugstores,
mail order
♥

Pro-Tec Pet Health
5440 Camus Rd.
Carson City, NV 89701-
9306
775-884-2566
800-44-FLEAS
www.protec-pet-health.com
Products companion animal
shampoo and vitamins
Availability companion
animal supply stores, health
food stores, mail order

Legend

♥ Vegan

■ Parent company does
not comply with
PETA's statement of
assurance

🛒 Products available
through PETAMall.com

Puig USA
70 E. 55th St.
New York, NY 10022
212-980-9620
www.puig.com
Products fragrance for men
and women, toiletries
Availability department
stores

Pulse Products
16310 Garfield Ave.
Paramount, CA 90723
800-477-8573
www.oneononebodycare.
com
Products massage oil, shaving
cream, shower gel, skin care
Availability health food
stores, mail order
♥

Pure & Basic Products
20633 Fordyce Ave.
Carson, CA 90810
310-900-4200
800-432-3787
www.pureandbasic.com
Products air freshener,
dandruff shampoo,
deodorant, hair care and
styling, household supply,
hypo-allergenic skin care for
men and women, shaving
supply, shower gel, soap
Availability beauty supply
stores, cooperatives, mail
order, salons

**PureOlogy Serious
Colour Care**
2010 Main St., Ste. 650
Irvine, CA 92614
800-331-1502
www.pureology.com
Products hair care and
styling
Availability beauty supply
stores, salons
♥

Pure Touch
P.O. Box 234
Glen Ellen, CA 95442
707-996-7817
800-442-7873
www.puretouch.net
Products aromatherapy,
fragrance for women,
massage oil/lotion
Availability distributors,
health food stores, mail
order, spas
♥

Queen Helene
100 Rose Ave.
Hempstead, NY 11550
516-538-4600
800-645-3752
www.queenhelene.com
Products bathing supply,
deodorant, foot care, hair
care and styling, skin care
Availability boutiques,
cooperatives, department
stores, discount department
stores, drugstores, health
food stores, mail order,
specialty stores,
supermarkets

Queen of Trees
9150 S. Willow Dr.
Tempe, AZ 85284
602-367-4463
www.queenoftrees.com
Products body care, holistic
health care
Availability Web site

Rachel Perry
15140 Keswick St.
Van Nuys, CA 91405-1012
818-886-0202
800-966-8888
www.rachelperry.net
Products lip care, massage
oil/lotion, shower gel, skin
care, sun care
Availability drugstores, health
food stores, mail order,
supermarkets

Radiant Hands
30707 Co Rd. 1
La Crescent, MN 55947
507-643-5167
Products deodorant, skin
care
Availability health food
stores, mail order
♥

Rainbow Brite
389 Fifth Ave., Ste. 1100
New York, NY 10016
212-779-0544
www.townleygirl.com
Products cosmetics, lip care,
nail care
Availability discount
department stores,
drugstores, supermarkets

**Rainbow Research
Corporation**
170 Wilbur Pl.
Bohemia, NY 11716
631-589-5563
800-722-9595
www.rainbowresearch.com
Products baby bathing
supply, bubble bath, hair care,
hair color, hypo-allergenic
skin care for men and
women, massage oil, soap
Availability boutiques,
cooperatives, drugstores,
health food stores, mail
order, specialty stores,
supermarkets

Recycline
681 Main St.
Waltham, MA 02451
781-893-1032
888-354-7296
www.recycline.com
Products razors,
toothbrushes
Availability health food
stores, Web site
♥

COMPANIES THAT
DON'T TEST ON ANIMALS

Rejuvi Laboratory, Inc.
360 Swift Ave., Ste. 38
S. San Francisco, CA 94080
650-588-7794
www.rejuvilab.com
Products hair care, massage
oil/lotion, skin care, sun care
Availability dermatologists,
mail order, salons, spas

Renée Rouleau
4025 Preston Rd., Ste. 606
Plano, TX 75093
972-248-6131
888-211-7560
www.reneerouleau.com
Products skin care, sun care
Availability mail order, Renée
Rouleau Store, Web site

Reviva Laboratories
705 Hopkins Rd.
Haddonfield, NJ 08033
856-428-3885
800-257-7774
www.revivalabs.com
Products bathing supply,
bleaching cream, body care,
cosmetics, hair care, herbal
supplements, hypo-allergenic
skin care for men and
women, makeup remover,
self-tanning lotion, soap,
sunburn relief, sun care
Availability boutiques,
cooperatives, discount
department stores,
distributors, drugstores,
health food stores, mail
order, supermarkets

Revlon
237 Park Ave.
New York, NY 10017
212-572-5000
800-473-8566
www.revlon.com
Products cosmetics,
deodorant, ethnic personal
care, hair care, hair color, nail
care, skin care, toiletries
Availability drugstores, mass
retailers, supermarkets

Rivers Run
6120 W. Tropicana A16-357
Las Vegas, NV 89103
702-252-3477
800-560-6753
www.riversrun.net
Products all-purpose cleaner,
car care, carpet cleaner,
companion animal shampoo,
glass cleaner, hypo-allergenic
skin care for men and
women, laundry detergent,
oven cleaner
Availability mail order, Rivers
Run stores, Web site
♥

Rodan + Fields
1550 Bryant St., Ste. 555
San Francisco, CA 94103
888-995-5656
www.rodanandfields.com
Products skin care
Availability department
stores, Web site

Royal Labs Natural
Cosmetics
P.O. Box 22434
Charleston, SC 29413
843-559-7541
800-760-7779
www.aromabella.com
Products acne treatment,
aromatherapy, bathing
supply, body care, body oils,
essential oils, foot care, hypo-
allergenic skin care for men
and women
Availability boutiques, health
food stores, mail order,
salons, skin clinics, spas,
specialty stores,
supermarkets
♥

Rusk
1 Cummings Point Rd.
Stamford, CT 06904
203-316-4300
800-USE-RUSK
www.rusk1.com
Products hair care and
styling, hair color, hair styling
tools, permanent waves
Availability salons

Safeway
5918 Stoneridge Mall Rd.
Pleasanton, CA 94588-3229
800-SAFEWAY
www.safeway.com
Products baby care,
household supply, toiletries
Availability Safeway
supermarkets

Sanford
2711 Washington Blvd.
Bellwood, IL 60104
708-547-6650
800-323-0749
www.sanfordcorp.com
Products art supply, ink,
office supply, writing
instruments
Availability department
stores, drugstores, mail order,
office supply stores,
supermarkets

Santa Fe Botanical
Fragrances
P.O. Box 282
Santa Fe, NM 87504
505-474-0302
Products aromatherapy,
fragrance for men and
women
Availability health food
stores, mail order
♥

The Santa Fe Soap Company
369 Montezuma, #167
Santa Fe, NM 87501
505-988-1122
888-762-7227
www.santafesoap.com
Products body care, hair care, shower gel, soap
Availability bath shops, boutiques, cooperatives, department stores, health food stores, independent sales representatives, mail order, specialty stores, supermarkets
♥

Sappo Hill Soapworks
654 Tolman Creek Rd.
Ashland, OR 97520
541-482-4485
800-863-7627
www.sappohill.com
Products soap
Availability cooperatives, drugstores, health food stores, supermarkets
♥

Scandia Spa
1900 Superior Ave., Ste. 209
Cleveland, OH 44114
216-932-4963
www.scandiaspa.com
Products bath salts, soap
Availability health food stores, mail order, Web site

Scents of Well Being
145 Hummingbird Ln.
Talent, OR 97540
800-355-8428
www.jackismagiclotion.com
Products body care, massage lotion
Availability cooperatives, health food stores, mail order, spas, Web site

Schiff Products
2002 S. 5070 W.
Salt Lake City, UT 84104
801-975-5000
800-444-5200
www.schiffvitamins.com
Products vitamin and mineral supplements
Availability health food stores, mail order

Scruples
8231 214th St. W.
Lakeville, MN 55044
952-469-4646
800-457-0016
www.scrupleshaircare.com
Products hair care and styling
Availability salons

SeaChi Organics
P.O. Box 4734
Palm Springs, CA 92263
760-320-3122
www.seachi.com
Products aromatherapy, bathing supply, body care, body oil, hair loss treatment, massage lotion
Availability health food stores, mail order, Web site

Sebastian International
429 Santa Monica Blvd.
Santa Monica, CA 90401
818-999-5112
800-829-7322
www.sebastian-intl.com
Products cosmetics, hair care, hair color, skin care
Availability salons
■

Secret Gardens
P.O. Box 449
N. San Juan, CA 95960
800-537-8766
Products air freshener, aromatherapy, bath salts, fragrance for men and women, massage oil/lotion
Availability boutiques, cooperatives, drugstores, health food stores, mail order, specialty stores
♥

Sensitille Naturals, Ltd.
#214-3495 Cambie St.
Vancouver, BC V5Z 4R3
Canada
604-879-2623
888-488-1808
www.sensitille.com
Products lubricants
Availability health food stores, supermarkets, Web site
♥

Serf to Surf Products
259 Hastings St. E.
Vancouver, BC V6A 1P2
Canada
604-669-2207
www.serftosurf.com
Products baby care, body care, companion animal care, healing salve, lip care
Availability health food stores, mail order, Serf to Surf store, Web site

COMPANIES THAT
DON'T TEST ON ANIMALS

SerVaas Laboratories
1100 Waterway Blvd.
Indianapolis, IN 46202
317-636-7760
800-433-5818
www.barkeepersfriend.com
Products all-purpose cleaner,
copper cleaner, cream
cleanser, oven cleaner,
powdered cleanser, stain
remover, toilet cleaner
Availability discount
department stores,
drugstores, supermarkets
♥

Seventh Generation
212 Battery St., Ste. A
Burlington, VT 05401
802-658-3773
www.seventhgen.com
Products all-purpose cleaner,
baby detergent and wipes,
bleach, carpet cleaner, cream
cleanser, diapers, dish
detergent, fabric softener,
glass cleaner, laundry
detergent, paper products,
toilet cleaner, trash bags
Availability cooperatives,
health food stores, mail
order, supermarkets, Web
site
♥

Shaklee Corporation
4747 Willow Rd.
Pleasanton, CA 94588
925-924-2000
800-SHAKLEE
www.shaklee.com
Products acne treatment,
aftershave lotion, all-purpose
cleaner, automatic
dishwashing detergent,
baby bathing supply, body
care, cosmetics, dandruff
shampoo, deodorant, dish
detergent, drain cleaner,
fabric softener, fragrance for
men and women, hair care
and styling, herbal
supplements, holistic health
care, hypo-allergenic skin
care, laundry detergent, lip
care, makeup remover,
shower gel, soap, sun care,
toothpaste, vitamins, water
filtration
Availability independent sales
representatives, Web site

Shaman Earthly Organics
5500 W. 83rd St.
Los Angeles, CA 90045
310-838-7543
877-JASON-01
www.shamanbeauty.com
Products hair care and
styling, shower gel, skin care
Availability health food
stores

ShiKai
P.O. Box 2866
Santa Rosa, CA 95405
707-544-0298
800-448-0298
www.shikai.com
Products body care, hair
care, henna hair color,
shower gel, skin care
Availability boutiques,
cooperatives, drugstores,
health food stores, mail
order, specialty stores

Silver Brights
1063 McGaw, Ste. 100
Irvine, CA 92614
949-794-5500
www.citreshine.com
Products hair care and
styling
Availability beauty supply
stores, drugstores,
supermarkets
■

Simplers Botanical Company
P.O. Box 2534
Sebastopol, CA 95472
707-887-2012
800-652-7646
www.simplers.com
Products aromatherapy,
essential oil, fragrance for
women, herbal extracts
Availability health food
stores, mail order, Web site
♥

Simple Wisdom
775 S. Graham
Memphis, TN 38111
901-458-4686
Products all-purpose
cleaner, diaper-rash
treatment, hair care, laundry
detergent, liquid soap, soap-
making supply, stain
remover
Availability cooperatives,
drugstores, health food
stores, mail order

Legend
♥ Vegan

■ Parent company does
not comply with
PETA's statement of
assurance

🛒 Products available
through PETAMall.com

COMPANIES THAT
DON'T TEST ON ANIMALS

Simply Soap
6721 Delfern St.
San Diego, CA 92120
619-287-1394
888-575-SOAP
www.simplysoap.com
Products soap
Availability mail order, Web
site
♥

Sinclair & Valentine
480 Airport Blvd.
Watsonville, CA 95076-2056
831-722-9526
800-563-2159
www.sinclairandvalentine.com
Products air freshener,
aromatherapy, bathing supply,
foot care, fragrance for
women, household supply, lip
care, massage oil, skin care
for women, soap, toiletries
Availability discount
department stores,
drugstores, independent
sales representatives,
supermarkets

Skinvac
1 Scotts Rd., #03-25
Shaw Centre
Singapore 228208
+65-67332579
www.skinvac.com
Products skin care
Availability health food
stores, Web site
♥

Smashbox Cosmetics
8538 Warner Dr.
Culver City, CA 90232
310-558-1490
888-763-1361
www.smashbox.com
Products cosmetics, hypo-
alergenic skin care, makeup
remover
Availability department
stores, mail order, QVC,
Smashbox stores, Web site

Smith & Vandiver
480 Airport Blvd.
Watsonville, CA 95076-2056
831-722-9526
800-722-1434
www.smith-vandiver.com
Products air freshener,
aromatherapy, baby care,
bathing supply, body care,
essential oils, foot care,
fragrance for women, hair
care, household supply, lip
care, massage oil, nail care,
shaving supply, skin care for
men and women, soap,
toiletries
Availability boutiques,
department stores, health
food stores, independent
sales representatives,
specialty stores

Smooth 'N Shine
1063 McGraw, Ste. 100
Irvine, CA 92614
949-794-5500
www.citreshine.com
Products hair care and
styling
Availability beauty supply
stores, drugstores,
supermarkets

The Soap Opera
319 State St.
Madison, WI 53703
608-251-4051
800-251-7627
www.thesoapopera.com
Products aromatherapy, body
care, bubble bath, essential
oil, fragrance for men and
women, glycerin soap, hair
care, makeup remover,
massage oil/lotion, shower
gel, soap-making supply
Availability mail order, The
Soap Opera store, Web site

Soapworks
18911 Nordhoff St., Ste. 37
Northridge, CA 91324
800-987-6564
www.soapworks.com
Products all-purpose cleaner,
bleach, laundry detergent
Availability drugstores, health
food stores, mail order,
Soapworks store,
supermarkets, Web site
♥

Sojourner Farms
Natural Pet Products
1 19th Ave. S.
Minneapolis, MN 55454
612-343-7262
888-867-6567
www.sojos.com
Products companion animal
care, food, supply, and
vitamins
Availability cooperatives,
health food stores, mail
order, specialty stores,
supermarkets

Solgar Vitamin Company
500 Willow Tree Rd.
Leonia, NJ 07605
201-944-2311
800-645-2246
www.solgar.com
Products vitamins
Availability cooperatives, health food stores

Sombra Cosmetics
5951 Office Blvd.
Albuquerque, NM 87109
505-888-0288
800-225-3963
www.sombrausa.com
Products body care, cosmetics, hand sanitizer, pain relief, skin care
Availability drugstores, health food stores, mail order

Sonoma Soap Company
1105 Industrial Ave.
Petaluma, CA 94952
707-769-5120
800-227-5120
www.avalonnaturalproducts.com
Products body care, glycerin soap, shower gel
Availability boutiques, health food stores, mail order, specialty stores, Web site

SoRik International
278 Talleyrand Ave.
Jacksonville, FL 32202
904-353-4200
Products hair care, sun care
Availability salons

Sound Earth, LLC
P.O. Box 245
Fishkill, NY 12524
845-489-2378
www.clearly-natural.com
Products air freshener, all-purpose cleaner, baby bathing supply, carpet cleaner, cream cleanser, floor cleaner, fruit and vegetable wash, furniture polish, powdered cleanser
Availability mail order, Web site
♥

Soya System
10441 Midwest Industrial
St. Louis, MO 63132
314-428-0004
www.soya.com
Products hair care and styling, permanent waves
Availability beauty supply stores, salons

Spring Rain Botanicals
P.O. Box 257
Fonthill, ON L0S 1E0
Canada
905-892-2944
www.springrainbotanicals.com
Products aromatherapy, baby bathing supply, body care, companion animal care, foot care, insect repellent, lip care, massage oil, pregnancy care, skin care, soap, sun care
Availability department stores, drugstores, health food stores, mail order, Web site.

Staedtler, Ltd.
Cowbridge Rd.
Pontyclym, Mid Glamorgan
Wales, Great Britain
011 44 14 4323 7421
Products office supply, writing instruments
Availability office supply stores in the U.K.

Stanley Home Products
67 Hunt St.
Agawam, MA 01001-1920
413-527-4001
800-628-9032
www.stanleyhome.com
Products all-purpose cleaner, bathroom cleaner, brass/copper/silver/stainless-steel cleaner, carpet cleaner, cosmetics, fine washables detergent, fragrance for men and women, furniture polish, glass cleaner, hair care, jewelry cleaner, laundry detergent, skin care, stain remover, vitamins
Availability independent sales representatives, Web site

Steel Cosmetics
P.O. Box 1372, Stn. B
Sudbury, ON P3E 5K4
Canada
705-662-2749
www.steelcosmetics.com
Products makeup remover, skin care
Availability Web site
♥

Stevens Research Salon Products
19417 63rd Ave. N.E.
Arlington, WA 98223
360-435-4513
800-262-3344
www.stevensresearch.com
Products aromatherapy, bath salts, body oil, hair care and styling, shower gel, skin care
Availability salons
♥

Stila Cosmetics
2801 Hyperion Ave.
Studio 102
Los Angeles, CA 90027
323-913-9443
www.stilacosmetics.com
Products cosmetics,
fragrance for women, lip
care, nail care, sun care
Availability department
stores

St. John's Botanicals
P.O. Box 100
Bowie, MD 20719
301-262-5302
www.stjohnsbotanicals.com
Products aromatherapy, bath
salts, body care, essential oil,
fragrance for men and
women, nutritional
supplements, shower gel,
soap
Availability drugstores, health
food stores, mail order

Strawberry Shortcake
389 Fifth Ave., Ste. 1100
New York, NY 10016
212-779-0544
www.townleygirl.com
Products cosmetics, lip care
Availability discount
department stores,
drugstores, supermarkets

Strong Products
2725 Hidden Hills Way
Corona, CA 92882
909-371-5185
800-648-9729
www.strongproducts.com
Products bathing supply, self-
tanning lotion
Availability Web site
♥

Studio Magic Cosmetics
20135 Cypress Creek Dr.
Alva, FL 33920-3305
239-728-3344
www.studiomagiccosmetics.c
om
Products cosmetics, lip care,
theatrical makeup
Availability boutiques,
independent sales
representatives, mail order,
physicians, spas, specialty
stores

Stuff by Hilary Duff
389 Fifth Ave., Ste. 1100
New York, NY 10016
212-779-0544
www.townleygirl.com
Products cosmetics, nail care
Availability discount
department stores,
drugstores, supermarkets

Sudz
P.O. Box 224, 144 Main St.
Gardiner, NY 12525
845-255-0844
800-262-KISS
www.organicsudz.com
Products liquid soap, shower
gel, soap
Availability boutiques,
cooperatives, drugstores,
health food stores, mail
order, massage therapists,
salons, Web site

Sukesha
P.O. Box 5126
Manchester, NH 03109
603-669-4228
800-221-3496
www.sukesha.com
Products hair care and
styling
Availability salons

Suki's, Inc.
P.O. Box 8
Northfield, MA 01360
413-498-5063
888-858-SUKI
www.sukisnaturals.com
Products aromatherapy, baby
care, bathing supply, body
care, fragrance for women,
hair care, lip care, personal
care, skin care
Availability boutiques, health
food stores, mail order,
salons, spas, Web site

Sumeru
1100 Lotus Dr.
Silver Lake, WI 53170
800-478-6378
Products aromatherapy, bath
salts, body care, massage
oil/lotion
Availability health food
stores, mail order
♥

Sun & Earth, Inc.
125 Noble St.
Norristown, PA 19401
800-298-7861
www.sunandearth.com
Products all-purpose cleaner,
dish detergent, fabric
softener, glass cleaner,
laundry detergent
Availability health food
stores, supermarkets, Web
site
♥

**SunFeather Natural
Soap Company**
1551 Hwy. 72
Potsdam, NY 13676
315-265-3648
www.sunsoap.com
Products aromatherapy,
candles, companion animal
shampoo, hair care, insect
repellent, soap, soap-making
supply
Availability boutiques,
cooperatives, department
stores, drugstores, health
food stores, independent
sales representatives, mail
order, specialty stores, Web
site

Sunrider International
1625 Abalone Ave.
Torrance, CA 90501
310-781-3808
www.sunrider.com
Products aftershave lotion,
body care, cosmetics, dental
hygiene, fragrance for women,
hair care, nail care, shaving
cream, shower gel, skin care,
soap, sun care, vitamins
Availability independent sales
representatives

**Sunshine Products
Group**
1616 Press Rd., Ste. 2B
Los Angeles, CA 98910
310-275-9891
800-285-6457
Products aromatherapy, body
care, essential oil, herbal
supplements, massage
oil/lotion
Availability drugstores, health
food stores, mail order
♥

**Supreme Beauty
Products Company**
820 S. Michigan
Chicago, IL 60605
312-322-0670
800-272-6602
Products hair care and styling
Availability drugstores, mail
order

Tammy Taylor Nails
18007E Skypark Cir., Ste. E
Irvine, CA 92614
949-250-9287
800-93-TAMMY
www.tammytaylornails.com
Products bathing supply,
body care, cosmetics, hair
care, hand sanitizer, massage
oil/lotion, nail care, self-
tanning lotion, sun care
Availability distributors, mail
order, Tammy Taylor stores

**TaUT by Leonard
Engelman**
P.O. Box 1870
Simi Valley, CA 93062-1870
805-522-8390
800-438-8288
www.tautcosmetics.com
Products body care,
cosmetics, foot care, hypo-
allergenic skin care for men
and women, lip care,
theatrical makeup
Availability beauty supply
stores, boutiques, health food
stores, mail order, salons,
specialty stores

Ted Baker Fragrance
304 Park Ave. S., 11th Fl.
New York, NY 10010
212-590-2471
www.shave.com
Products deodorant, body
care, body wash, fragrance
for men and women, skin
care for men and women,
shaving supply
Availability salons, spas,
specialty stores, Web site

TerraNova
1011 Gilman St.
Berkeley, CA 94710
510-558-7100
800-966-3457
www.terranovabody.com
Products bath salts, body
care, fragrance for women,
glycerin soap, shower gel
Availability boutiques,
department stores, specialty
stores

Terressentials
2650 Old National Pike
Middletown, MD 21769-
8817
301-371-7333
www.terressentials.com
Products baby bathing
supply, body care, deodorant,
hair care, lip care, shower
gel, skin care, soap
Availability boutiques, health
food stores, mail order,
specialty stores, Terressentials
stores, Web site

That's So Raven
389 Fifth Ave., Ste. 1100
New York, NY 10016
212-779-0544
www.townleygirl.com
Products cosmetics, lip care,
nail care
Availability discount
department stores,
drugstores, supermarkets

Thicker Fuller Hair
1063 McGaw, Ste. 100
Irvine, CA 92614
949-794-5500
www.citreshine.com
Products hair care and
styling
Availability beauty supply
stores, drugstores,
supermarkets

■

Thursday Plantation
P.O. Box 1297
Summerland, CA 93067-
1297
800-645-9500
Products dandruff shampoo,
dental hygiene, hair care,
hypo-allergenic skin care for
men and women, sun care,
toiletries
Availability drugstores, health
food stores, supermarkets

Tish & Snooky's Manic
Panic NYC
(Tish & Snooky's)
2107 Borden Ave., 4th Fl.
Long Island City, NY 11101
718-937-6055
800-95-MANIC
www.manicpanic.com
Products cosmetics, false
eyelashes, hair bleach, hair
color, hair styling, nail care,
wigs
Availability drugstores, health
food stores, mail order,
specialty boutiques, Web site

Tommy Hilfiger
372 W. Broadway
New York, NY 10012
917-237-0983
www.tommy.com
Products aftershave lotion,
bathing supply, body care,
deodorant, fragrance for
men and women, hair care,
skin care
Availability department
stores

Tom's of Maine
P.O. Box 710
302 Lafayette Ctr.
Kennebunk, ME 04043
207-985-2944
800-367-8667
www.tomsofmaine.com
Products dental floss,
deodorant, mouthwash,
shaving cream, soap,
toothpaste
Availability boutiques,
cooperatives, drugstores,
health food stores, mail
order, specialty stores,
supermarkets, Tom's of
Maine store, Web site

Too Faced Cosmetics
17595 Harvard, Ste. C-503
Irvine, CA 92614
949-553-4431
www.toofaced.com
Products cosmetics, lip care,
nail care
Availability department
stores, mail order, Web site

Tova Corporation
192 N. Canon Dr.
Beverly Hills, CA 90210
310-246-0218
800-852-9999
www.beautybytova.com
Products cosmetics,
fragrance for men and
women, shower gel, skin
care, soap
Availability boutiques,
department stores

Trader Joe's Company
P.O. Box 5049
Monrovia, CA 91017
800-SHOP-TJS
www.traderjoes.com
Products hair care, herbal
supplements, household
supply, toiletries, vitamins
Availability Trader Joe's
Company stores

Tressa
P.O. Box 75320
Cincinnati, OH 45275
859-525-1300
800-879-8737
www.tressa.com
Products hair bleach, hair
care and styling, hair color,
permanent waves
Availability salons

TRI Hair Care Products
13918 Equitable Rd.
Cerritos, CA 90703
562-926-7373
866-644-7373
www.trihaircare.com
Products body care, hair care
and styling
Availability boutiques, mail
order, specialty stores

Tyra Skin Care
20520 Hiawatha St.
Chatsworth, CA 91311
818-407-1274
800-322-TYRA
www.tyraskincare.com
Products body care,
cosmetics, hypo-allergenic
skin care for men and
women, shower gel
Availability boutiques,
department stores, mail
order, specialty stores

The Ultimate Life
P.O. Box 4308
Santa Barbara, CA 93140
800-843-6325
www.ultimatelife.com
Products nutritional bars,
powders, shakes/drinks,
supplements
Availability health food
stores, mail order
♥

Ultima II (Revlon)
625 Madison Ave.
New York, NY 10022
212-572-5000
Products cosmetics
Availability department
stores

Unicure
TSI, P.O. Box 1222
Hendersonville, TN 37077
888-UNICURE
www.unicure.com
Products hair care and
styling
Availability department
stores, drugstores, mail order,
Unicure stores, Web site

Un-Petroleum Lip Care
1105 Industrial Ave.
Petaluma, CA 94952
707-347-1200
800-227-5120
www.avalonorganics.com
Products body care, lip care
Availability health food
stores, mail order, Web site

**Upper Canada Soap &
Candle Makers**
1510 Caterpillar Rd.
Mississauga, ON L4X 2W9
Canada
905-897-1710
www.uppercanadasoap.com
Products air freshener, body
care, bubble bath, candles,
dish detergent, hand sanitizer,
liquid soap, shower gel
Availability gift stores

Urban Decay
729 Farad St.
Costa Mesa, CA 92627
949-631-4504
800-784-URBAN
www.urbandecay.com
Products bathing supply,
body care, cosmetics,
fragrance for women, nail
care, theatrical makeup,
vegan makeup brushes
Availability boutiques,
discount department stores,
mail order, specialty stores

USA King's Crossing
P.O. Box 832074
Richardson, TX 75083
972-801-9473
800-SHAV-KNG
www.shaveking.com
Products razors, shaving
supply
Availability cooperatives,
drugstores, health food
stores, mail order
♥

Vermont Soapworks
616 Exchange St.
Middlebury, VT 05753
802-388-4302
www.vermontsoap.com
Products all-purpose cleaner,
aromatherapy, baby bathing
supply, bath salts, fruit and
vegetable wash, liquid soap,
shower gel, soap
Availability boutiques,
cooperatives, department
stores, drugstores, health
food stores, mail order,
specialty stores, Vermont
Soapworks stores

Vernacular Skinworks
2008 Englewood Ave.
Durham, NC 27705
919-416-4830
www.vernacularskinworks.com
Products skin care
Availability Web site

COMPANIES THAT
DON'T TEST ON ANIMALS

Veterinarian's Best
P.O. Box 4459
Santa Barbara, CA 93103
805-963-5609
800-866-PETS
www.vetsbest.com
Products companion animal shampoo and vitamins
Availability companion animal supply stores, health food stores, mail order, specialty stores, supermarkets

Victoria's Secret
P.O. Box 16589
Columbus, OH 43216-6589
800-411-5116
www.victoriassecret.com
Products body care, cosmetics, fragrance for women, lip care, makeup remover, skin care, sun care
Availability mail order, Victoria's Secret stores

Virginia's Soap
Box 45033 RPO
Regent, Winnipeg, MB
R2C 5C7
Canada
204-222-5492
800-563-6127
Products aromatherapy, bathing supply, soap
Availability boutiques, mail order, specialty stores

Von Natur
P.O. Box 33761
Portland, OR 97292
503-722-7557
www.vonnatur.com
Products aromatherapy, bathing supply, body care, foot care, hair care, massage oil, pain relief, scar gel, shaving supply, skin care
Availability boutiques, department stores, health food stores, mail order, Von Natur store, Web site

V'TAE Parfum & Body Care
569 Searls Ave.
Nevada City, CA 95959
530-265-4255
800-643-3011
www.vtae.com
Products aromatherapy, baby care and bathing supply, bath salts, body care, bubble bath, companion animal care, foot care, fragrance for women, insect repellent, lip care, massage oil, nail care, shower gel, soap, sunburn relief
Availability boutiques, cooperatives, department stores, health food stores, mail order, specialty stores, V'tae Parfum & Body Care stores
☞

Wachters' Organic Sea Products
550 Sylvan St.
Daly City, CA 94014
650-757-9851
800-682-7100
www.wachters.com
Products all-purpose cleaner, ayurvedic supply, companion animal vitamins, herbal supplements, holistic health care, laundry detergent, nutritional shakes, vitamins
Availability independent sales representatives, mail order
♥

Warm Earth Cosmetics
1155 Stanley Ave.
Chico, CA 95928-6944
530-895-0455
www.geocities.com/warmearthcosmetics
Products cosmetics
Availability boutiques, department stores, health food stores, independent sales representatives, mail order, specialty stores

Watkins Incorporated
150 Liberty St.
P.O. Box 5570
Winona, MN 55987-0570
507-457-3300
800-243-9423
www.watkinsonline.com
Products air fresheners, all-purpose cleaner, aromatherapy, automatic dishwashing detergent, bathing supply, bathroom cleaner, body care, candles, carpet cleaner, companion animal shampoo, cream cleanser, deodorant, drain opener, fabric softener, foot care, fruit and vegetable wash, furniture polish, glass cleaner, hair care, laundry detergent, lip care, mouthwash, shaving supply, skin care, toothpaste
Availability independent sales representatives, Web site

Weleda
1 Closer Rd.
Palisades, NY 10964
845-268-8599
www.weleda.com
Products baby care, bathing supply, body care, body oil, deodorant, foot care, hair care, herbal supplements, holistic health care, lip care, massage oil/lotion, shaving cream, skin care, soap, toothpaste
Availability boutiques, cooperatives, drugstores, health food stores, mail order, specialty stores, Weleda store

The Wella Corporation
6109 De Soto
Woodland Hills, CA 91367
800-526-4657
www.wella.com
Products ethnic personal
care, hair care, hair color,
permanent waves
Availability boutiques, salons,
specialty stores
■

Well-in-Hand
5164 Waterlick Rd.
Forest, VA 24551-1200
434-534-6050
888-550-7774
www.wellinhand.com
Products acne treatment,
aromatherapy, baby care,
bathing supply, deodorant,
essential oil, feminine
hygiene, first aid, herbal
supplements, holistic health
care, lice treatment, pain
relief, skin care, soap, wart
treatment
Availability drugstores, health
food stores, mail order, Web
site
♥

Whip-It Products
P.O. Box 30128
Pensacola, FL 32503
850-626-6300
800-582-0398
Products all-purpose cleaner
for home and industrial use,
carpet cleaner, household
supply, laundry detergent,
oven cleaner
Availability independent sales
representatives, mail order
♥

White Acres Farm, Inc.
765 Astral Pt.
Spring Branch, TX 78070
830-935-3306
800-449-7071
www.whiteacresfarm.com
Products insect repellent,
skin care
Availability health food
stores, mail order,
supermarkets, Web site

**Whole Spectrum
Aromatherapy**
6710 Benjamin Rd., Ste. 700
Tampa, FL 33634
813-886-9698
www.wholespectrum.biz
Products aromatherapy,
bubble bath, essential oil,
fragrance for women, hair
care, hypo-allergenic skin
care, massage oil/lotion,
nonprescription therapy,
shower gel, soap
Availability boutiques, health
care centers, health food
stores, mail order, salons,
spas, specialty stores, Web
site
♥

Wind River Herbs
P.O. Box 3673
Alphine, WY 83128
307-883-7070
800-903-4372
www.windriverherbs.com
Products body care, body oil,
herbal supplements, holistic
health care, insect repellant,
lip care
Availability health food
stores, The Herb Store, mail
order

WiseWays Herbals
Singing Brook Farm
99 Harvey Rd.
Worthington, MA 01098
413-238-4268
888-540-1600
www.wiseways.com
Products air freshener,
aromatherapy, baby care,
bathing supply, deodorant,
feminine hygiene, furniture
polish, hair care, insect
repellent, lip care, skin care,
soap, sun care
Availability boutiques,
cooperatives, department
stores, drugstores, health
food stores, mail order,
specialty stores

Womankind
E3101 Tewalt Rd.
De Soto, WI 54624
608-648-2316
www.mwt.net/~womankind
Products feminine hygiene
Availability boutiques,
cooperatives, health food
stores, independent sales
representatives, mail order,
specialty stores,
supermarkets, Web site

W.S. Badger
P.O. Box 58
Gilsum, NH 03488
800-603-6100
www.badgerbalm.com
Products aromatherapy, baby
care, insect repellant, lip
balm, massage oil, skin care,
sun care
Availability department
stores, drugstores, health
food stores, mail order, Web
site

Wysong Corporation
1880 N. Eastman Rd.
Midland, MI 48642-7779
989-631-0009
800-748-0188
www.wysong.net
Products air freshener,
companion animal care,
dental hygiene, deodorant,
equine products, hair care,
self-tanning lotion, shaving
gel, skin care, sun care,
vitamins
Availability health food
stores, mail order

XCD
304 Park Ave. S., 11th Fl.
New York, NY 10010
212-590-2471
www.xcdskn.com
Products skin care for men
Availability drugstores, health
food stores, mail order,
supermarkets, Web site

Xeno Company
2683 Timberbrooke Pl.
Duluth, GA 30097
404-918-7788
www.xenocompany.com
Products aromatherapy,
candles, soap
Availability Web site
♥

ZENMED
240-1555 McKenzie Ave.
Victoria, BC V8N 1A4
Canada
250-382-7243
877-647-4242
www.zenmed.com
Products acne treatment,
body care, fragrance, rosacea
treatment, scar gel, skin care
Availability health food
stores, mail order, Web site
♥

Zero Frizz
1063 McGaw, Ste. 100
Irvine, CA 92614
949-794-5500
www.citreshine.com
Products hair care and
styling products
Availability beauty supply
stores, drugstores,
supermarkets

Zia Natural Skincare
1337 Evans Ave.
San Francisco, CA 94124
415-642-8339
800-334-7546
www.zianatural.com
Products acne treatment,
aromatherapy, body care,
cosmetics, self-tanning lotion,
skin care, sun care
Availability boutiques,
cooperatives, health food
stores, mail order, specialty
stores, Web site

Zuzu Cosmetics
P.O. Box 50130
Bellevue, WA 98015
800-497-6419
www.gabrielcosmeticsinc.
com
Products cosmetics
Availability health food
stores, mail order,
supermarkets

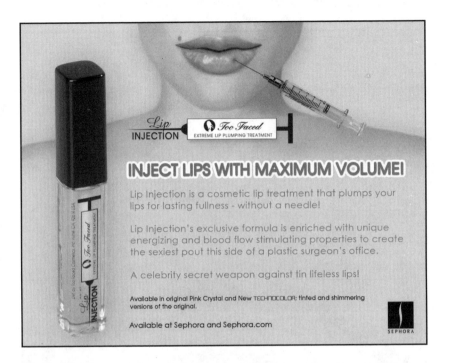

QUICK REFERENCE
GUIDE

QUICK REFERENCE GUIDE

QUICK REFERENCE GUIDE

QUICK REFERENCE GUIDE

QUICK REFERENCE GUIDE

QUICK REFERENCE GUIDE

QUICK REFERENCE GUIDE

Makeup Brushes (Vegan)

QUICK REFERENCE GUIDE

QUICK REFERENCE GUIDE

QUICK REFERENCE GUIDE

QUICK REFERENCE GUIDE

QUICK REFERENCE GUIDE

COMPANIES THAT
DO TEST ON ANIMALS ▰▰▰▰▰▰▰▰

Why Are These Companies Included on the 'Do Test' List?

The following companies manufacture products that are tested on animals.
Those marked with a check (✓) are currently observing a moratorium
on (i.e., current suspension of) animal testing. Please encourage them to
announce a permanent ban. Listed in parentheses are examples of products
manufactured either by that company or, if applicable, by its parent company.
For a complete listing of products manufactured by a company on this list,
please visit the company's Web site or contact it directly for more
information. Companies on this list may manufacture individual lines of
products without using animal tests (e.g., Clairol claims that its Herbal
Essences line is not tested on animals). They have not, however, eliminated
animal testing on their entire line of cosmetics and household products.

Similarly, companies on this list may make some products, such as
pharmaceuticals, that are required by law to be tested on animals. However,
the reason for these companies' inclusion is not the required animal testing
that they conduct, but rather the animal testing of personal care and
household products that is not required by law.

What Can Be Done About Animal Tests That Are Required by Law?

Although animal testing of pharmaceuticals and certain chemicals is still
mandated by law, the arguments against using animals for cosmetics testing
are also valid when applied to the pharmaceutical and chemical industries.
These industries are regulated by the Food and Drug Administration and
the Environmental Protection Agency, respectively, and it is the responsibility
of the companies that kill animals in order to bring their products to market
to convince the regulatory agencies that there are better ways to determine
product safety. PETA is actively working on this front by funding development
and validation of non-animal test methods and providing input through our
involvement on government advisory committees at both the national and
international levels. Companies resist progress because the crude nature of
animal tests allows them to market many products that might be determined
to be too toxic if cell culture tests were used. Let companies know how you
feel about this.

COMPANIES THAT
DO TEST ON ANIMALS

Arm & Hammer
(Church & Dwight)
P.O. Box 1625
Horsham, PA 19044-6625
800-524-1328
www.armhammer.com

Bic Corporation
500 Bic Dr.
Milford, CT 06460
203-783-2000
www.bicworld.com
✓

Boyle-Midway
(Reckitt Benckiser)
2 Wickman Rd.
Toronto, ON M8Z 5M5
Canada
416-255-2300

Braun
(Gillette Co.)
400 Unicorn Park Dr.
Woburn, MA 01801
800-272-8611
www.braun.com
✓

Chesebrough-Ponds
(Fabergé, Ponds, Vaseline)
800 Sylvan Ave.
Englewood Cliffs, NJ 07632
800-743-8640
www.pondssquad.com

Church & Dwight
(Aim, Arm & Hammer, Arrid,
Brillo, Close-Up, Lady's
Choice, Nair, Mentadent,
Pearl Drops)
P.O. Box 1625
Horsham, PA 19044-6625
800-524-1328
www.churchdwight.com

Clairol (Aussie, Daily
Defense, Herbal Essences,
Infusium 23, Procter &
Gamble)
1Blachley Rd.
Stamford, CT 06922
800-252-4765
www.clairol.com

Clorox (ArmorAll, Formula
409, Fresh Step, Glad, Liquid
Plumber, Pine-Sol, Soft Scrub,
S.O.S., Tilex)
1221 Broadway
Oakland, CA 94612
510-271-7000
800-227-1860
www.clorox.com

**Colgate-Palmolive
Company**
(Ajax, Fab, Hills Pet Nutrition,
Mennen, Palmolive, SoftSoap,
Speed Stick)
300 Park Ave.
New York, NY 10022
212-310-2000
800-221-4607
www.colgate.com

Coty (Adidas fragrance,
Calvin Klein, Davidoff, The
Healing Garden, Kenneth
Cole, Glow, Joop!, Jovan,
Lancaster, Marc Jacob,
Rimmel, Stetson)
237 Park Ave., 19th Fl.
New York, NY 10017-3142
212-389-7000
www.coty.com

Cover Girl
(Procter & Gamble)
1 Procter & Gamble Plz.
Cincinnati, OH 45202
513-983-1100
800-543-1745
www.covergirl.com

Del Laboratories
(Corn Silk, LaCross,
Naturistics, New York Color,
Propa PH, Sally Hansen)
178 EAB Plz.
Uniondale, NY 11556
516-844-2020
800-952-5080
www.dellabs.com

Dial Corporation
(Purex, Renuzit)
15101 N. Scottsdale Rd.
Ste. 5028
Scottsdale, AZ 85254-2199
800-528-0849
www.dialcorp.com

Erno Laszlo
3202 Queens Blvd.
Long Island City, NY 11101
718-729-4480
www.ernolaszlo.com

Gillette Co.
(Braun, Duracell)
Prudential Tower Bldg.
Boston, MA 02199
617-421-7000
800-872-7202
www.gillette.com
✓

Helene Curtis Industries
(Finesse, Salon Selectives,
Thermasilk, Unilever)
800 Sylvan Ave.
Englewood Cliffs, NJ 07632
800-621-2013
www.helenecurtis.com

Johnson & Johnson
(Aveeno, Clean & Clear,
Neutrogena, ROC)
1 Johnson & Johnson Plz.
New Brunswick, NJ 08933
732-524-0400
800-526-3967
www.jnj.com

**Kimberly-Clark
Corporation** (Cottonelle,
Huggies, Kleenex, Kotex, Pull-
Ups, Scott Paper)
P.O. Box 619100
Dallas, TX 75261-9100
800-544-1847
www.kimberly-clark.com

Lever Brothers
(Unilever)
800 Sylvan Ave.
Englewood Cliffs, NJ 07632
212-888-1260
800-598-1223
www.unilever.com

L'Oréal (Biotherm,
Cacharel, Garnier, Giorgio
Armani, Helena Rubinstein,
Lancôme, Matrix, Maybelline,
Ralph Lauren, Redken, Soft
Sheen, Vichy)
575 Fifth Ave.
New York, NY 10017
212-818-1500
www.lorealcosmetics.com

Max Factor
(Procter & Gamble)
1 Procter & Gamble Plz.
Cincinnati, OH 45202
513-983-1100
800-543-1745
www.maxfactor.com

Mead
10 W. 2nd St., #1
Dayton, OH 45402
937-495-6323
www.meadweb.com

Melaleuca
3910 S. Yellowstone Hwy.
Idaho Falls, ID 83402-6003
800-742-2444
www.melaleuca.com

Mennen Company
(Colgate-Palmolive)
191 E. Hanover Ave.
Morristown, NJ 07960-3151
973-631-9000
www.colgate.com

Neoteric Cosmetics
4880 Havana St.
Denver, CO 80239-0019
303-373-4860

New Dana Perfumes
470 Oakhill Rd.
Crestwood Industrial Park
Mountaintop, PA 18707
800-822-8547

Noxell (Procter & Gamble)
11050 York Rd.
Hunt Valley, MD 21030-2098
410-785-7300
800-572-3232
www.pg.com

**Olay Company/Oil of
Olay** (Procter & Gamble)
P.O. Box 599
Cincinnati, OH 45201
800-543-1745
www.oilofolay.com

Oral-B
(Gillette Company)
600 Clipper Dr.
Belmont, CA 94002-4119
415-598-5000
www.oralb.com
✓

Pantene
(Procter & Gamble)
1 Procter & Gamble Plz.
Cincinnati, OH 45202
800-945-7768
www.pantene.com

Pfizer (BenGay, Desitin,
Listerine, Lubriderm, Plax,
Visine)
235 E. 42nd St.
New York, NY 10017-5755
212-573-2323
www.pfizer.com

Physique
(Procter & Gamble)
1 Procter & Gamble Plz.
Cincinnati, OH 45202
800-214-8957
www.physique.com

Playtex Products
(Baby Magic, Banana Boat,
Olgilvie)
300 Nyala Farms Rd.
Westport, CT 06880
203-341-4000
www.playtex.com

Procter & Gamble Co.
(Clairol, Cover Girl, Crest,
Giorgio, Iams, Max Factor,
Physique, Tide)
1 Procter & Gamble Plz.
Cincinnati, OH 45202
513-983-1100
800-543-1745
www.pg.com

Reckitt Benckiser
(Easy Off, Lysol, Mop & Glo,
Old English, Resolve, Spray
'N Wash, Veet, Woolite)
1655 Valley Rd.
Wayne, NJ 07474-0945
201-633-6700
800-232-9665
www.reckittbenckiser.com

Richardson-Vicks
(Procter & Gamble)
1 Procter & Gamble Plz.
Cincinnati, OH 45202
513-983-1100
800-543-1745
www.pg.com

COMPANIES THAT
DO TEST ON ANIMALS

Sally Hansen
(Del Laboratories)
178 EAB Plz.
Uniondale, NY 11556
800-953-5080
www.sallyhansen.com

Schering-Plough (Bain
de Soleil, Coppertone, Dr.
Scholl's)
1 Giralda Farms
Madison, NJ 07940-1000
201-822-7000
800-842-4090
www.sch-plough.com

S.C. Johnson (Drano, Edge,
Fantastik, Glade, OFF!, Oust,
Pledge, Scrubbing Bubbles,
Shout, Skintimate, Windex,
Ziploc)
1525 Howe St.
Racine, WI 53403
414-260-2000
800-494-4855
www.scjohnson.com

SoftSoap Enterprises
(Colgate-Palmolive)
300 Park Ave.
New York, NY 10022
800-221-4607
www.colgate.com

Suave (Unilever)
800 Sylvan Ave.
Englewood Cliffs, NJ 07632
212-888-1260
800-782-8301
www.suave.com

3M (Post-It, Scotch)
3M Center
St. Paul, MN 55144-1000
651-733-1110
800-364-3577
www.3m.com

Unilever (Axe, Dove, Helene
Curtis, Lever Bros., Suave)
800 Sylvan Ave.
Englewood Cliffs, NJ 07632
212-888-1260
800-598-1223
www.unilever.com

✓ Companies with this mark are currently observing a moratorium on animal testing.

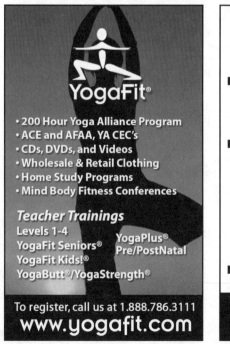

Bath-and-Body.com
1021 Bay Blvd., Ste. S
Chula Vista, CA 91911
619-425-0829
888-935-BODY
www.bath-and-body.com
Products bath bombs, bath
salts, body care, massage
oil/lotion, soap
Availability Web site

Cari Amici
5837 S. New York Ave.
Cudahy, WI 53110
414-769-1380
www.cariamici.net
Products air freshener, baby
bathing supply, baby wipes,
bathing supply, body care,
candles, companion animal
care, cosmetics, dental
hygiene, deodorant, diapers,
eye care, fragrance for
women, hair care, household
supply, shaving supply, shower
gel, skin care, soap, sun care
Availability Web site

Compassion Matters
2 E. Fourth St.
Jamestown, NY 14701
716-664-2207
800-422-6330
www.compassionmatters.com
Products air fresheners,
aromatherapy, baby care,
bathing supply, cosmetics,
dandruff shampoo, dental
hygiene, deodorant, dish
detergent, feminine hygiene,
hair care, household supply,
insect repellent, laundry
detergent, lip care, skin care,
soap, sun care
Availability Compassion
Matters store, mail order

A Different Daisy
10766 S.R. 139
Minford, OH 45653
740-820-3146
www.differentdaisy.com
Products air freshener,
aromatherapy, baby care,
bleach, companion animal
care, condoms/lubricants,
contact lens solutions,
cosmetics, dental hygiene,
deodorant, feminine hygiene,
furniture polish, hair care, hair
color, insect repellent, laundry
detergent, nail care, shaving
supply, skin care, sun care,
toothbrushes, vitamins
Availability mail order, Web
site

FaunaFree
310-664-6776
www.Faunafree.com
Products body care, foot
care, skin care, soap
Availability Web site

Green Earth Office
Supply
59 N. Santa Cruz Ave.
Los Gatos, CA 95030
408-395-3975
800-327-8449
www.greenearthofficesupply.
com
Products art supply, glue,
office supply
Availability mail order, Web
site

A Happy Planet
2261 Market St., #71
San Francisco, CA 94114
888-946-4277
www.ahappyplanet.com
Products bedding, household
supply, office supply,
T-shirts, undergarments
Availability mail order, Web
site

The Heritage Store
P.O. Box 444
Virginia Beach, VA 23458
757-428-0100
800-862-2923
www.caycecures.com
Products aromatherapy,
dandruff shampoo, dental
hygiene, essential oil,
fragrance, hair care, herbal
supplements, holistic health
care, hypo-allergenic skin
care, sun care, vitamins
Availability health food
stores, Heritage store, mail
order, Web site

InterNatural
P.O. Box 1008
Silver Lake, WI 53170
262-889-8501
800-643-4221
www.internatural-alternative-
health.com
Products aromatherapy,
condoms, cosmetics, dandruff
shampoo, dental hygiene,
feminine hygiene, furniture
polish, hair color, insect
repellent, laundry detergent,
nail care, skin care, sun care
Availability mail order, Web
site

Kid Bean
2400 N.E. 10th Ave.
Pompano Beach, FL 33064
www.kidbean.com
954-942-2830
Products all-purpose cleaner,
baby care, bleach, carpet
care, feminine hygiene, fruit
and vegetable wash, hair
care, household supply,
laundry detergent, skin care,
sun care, toothpaste
Availability Web site

CATALOGS/ONLINE STORES THAT OFFER
CRUELTY-FREE PRODUCTS

One Stop Vegan Shop
236 W. Main St.
Stilman Valley, IL 61084
815-978-1954
www.onestopveganshop.com
Products air freshner, baby
bathing supply, baby
detergent, baby wipes,
bleach, body care, candles,
carpet care, cleaning supply,
cosmetics, dandruff
shampoo, deodorant,
diapers, feminine hygiene,
hair care, razors, shaving
supply, soap, toothbrushes,
toothpaste
Availability Web site

Pangea Vegan Products
2381 Lewis Ave.
Rockville, MD 20851
800-340-1200
www.veganstore.com
Products baby care, clothing,
companion animal care,
cosmetics, dental hygiene,
feminine hygiene, hair care,
household supply, laundry
detergent, nail care, razors,
shoes, skin care, sun care,
toothbrushes, vegan
chocolate and snacks, vegan
food, vitamins
Availability mail order, Pangea
store, Web site
♥ ⊟

PETA
501 Front St.
Norfolk, VA 23510
757-622-7382
www.PETACatalog.com
Products household supply,
laundry detergent, razors,
soap
Availability mail order, PETA
Mall (www.PETAMall.com),
PETA Merchandise
Department
♥

Physicians Laboratories
(Revival Soy)
138 Oakwood Dr.
Winston-Salem, NC 27103
336-722-2337
800-500-2055
www.revivalhealth.com
Products herbal supplements,
soy coffee, soy protein
Availability mail order, Web
site

Sunrise Lane
780 Greenwich St.
Dept. PT
New York, NY 10014
212-242-7014
Products baby care, bathing
supply, bleach, carpet cleaner,
companion animal care,
dental hygiene, deodorant,
dish detergent, floor cleaner,
furniture polish, glass cleaner,
hair care, hair color, humane
mouse traps, hypo-allergenic
skin care, laundry detergent,
lip care, permanent waves,
shaving supply, soap
Availability mail order

VeganCats.com
1207 N. 43rd St.
Seattle, WA 98103
877-376-9056
www.vegancats.com
Products companion animal
care: accessories, dietary
supplements, flea control,
litter/waste disposal,
stain/odor remover, vegan
food/treats
Availability mail order, Web
site
♥

Vegan Mercantile
1207 N. 43rd St.
Seattle, WA 98103
877-376-9056
www.veganmercantile.com
Products air freshener, all-
purpose cleaner, baby care,
bathing supply, companion
animal care,
condoms/lubricants, contact
lens solutions, cosmetics,
dental hygiene, deodorant,
feminine hygiene, hair care,
household supply, insect
repellent, laundry detergent,
shaving supply, skin care, sun
care, vegan chocolate and
snacks, vegan food, vegan
makeup brushes
Availability mail order, Web
site
♥

Vegan Erotica
P.O. Box 2762
Salt Lake City, UT 84110
801-560-8238
www.veganerotica.com
Products condoms
Availability mail order, Web
site
♥

Vegan Essentials
3707 N. 92nd St.
Milwaukee, WI 53222
414-607-1953
866-88-VEGAN
www.veganessentials.com
Products air freshener, all-purpose cleaner, baby care, clothing, cosmetics, dental hygiene, deodorant, fragrance for women, glass cleaner, hair care, insect repellent, lip care, self-tanning lotion, shaving supply, shoe polish, shoes, skin care, sun care, vegan chocolate and snacks, vegan companion animal food, vegan food, vegan makeup brushes
Availability mail order
♥

Wow-Bow Distributors
13B Lucon Dr.
Deer Park, NY 11729
800-326-0230
www.wow-bow.com
Products companion animal care and biscuits, insect repellent, vegan and vegetarian food, vitamins
Availability mail order, Wow-Bow Distributors store

White Rabbit Beauty
P.O. Box 64
Lake Oswego, OR 97034
503-636-4630
888-312-3266
www.whiterabbitbeauty.com
Products baby care, cosmetics, hair care, nail care, self-tanning lotion, skin care, sun care
Availability Web site
🛒

COMPANION-ANIMAL
FOOD MANUFACTURERS

What's Wrong With 'Pet' Food?

Most caring consumers would never guess that lonely animals are confined to tiny, barren laboratory cages for years on end and subjected to horrible experiments in order to test dog and cat food. •

To expose this tragedy, PETA conducted a nine-month undercover investigation of a laboratory that performed cruel animal tests for Iams and other major companion-animal food companies.

What our investigator uncovered would outrage anyone with a heart:

■ Lonely dogs driven mad from confinement to barren steel and cement cells

■ Dogs dumped on cold concrete flooring after having chunks of muscle cut out of their thighs

■ Dogs with thier vocal cords severed in order to keep them quiet

■ Sick dogs left without veterinary care

These animals suffered so that Iams and other companion-animal food companies could slap "new and improved" labels on their products.

The following companies make top-quality food for dogs and cats—without harming animals in laboratories. Please help us save thousands of animals from unspeakable cruelty by buying only from these companies.

For more information about how dog and cat food is contaminated with cruelty and to find the most up-to-date list of companies that don't test on animals, check out IamsCruelty.com.

Companies listed have signed a PETA statement of assurance. Companies not on this list either responded that they do conduct laboratory experiments on animals or failed to respond to our numerous inquiries and are assumed to conduct laboratory experiments on animals. We recommend that you contact companies that are not included on this list and request that they respond to PETA's survey (available online) and/or provide you directly with more information about how their products are tested.

COMPANION-ANIMAL
FOOD MANUFACTURERS

Active Life Pet Products
877-291-2913
www.activelifepp.com

Amoré Pet Services, Inc.
866-572-6673
www.amorepetfoods.com

Animal Food Services
800-743-0322
www.animalfood.com

Artemis Pet Food
800-282-5876
www.artemiscompany.com

Azmira Holistic Animal Care
800-497-5665
www.azmira.com

Burns Pet Nutrition
877-983-9651
www.burns-pet-nutrition.co.uk

Canusa International
519-624-5697
www.canusaint.com

CountryPet Pet Food
800-454-7387
www.countrypet.com

Dr. Harvey's
866-362-4123
www.drharveys.com

Dry Fork Milling Co.
800-346-1360

Dynamite Marketing, Inc.
208-887-9410
www.dynamitemarketing.com

Evanger's Dog and Cat Food Co., Inc.
800-288-6796
www.evangersdogfood.com

Evolution Diet, Inc.
(entirely vegan)
800-659-0104
www.petfoodshop.com

Flint River Ranch
800-704-5779
www.flintriver-home.com

Good Dog Foods, Inc.
732-842-4555
www.gooddogfoods.com

GreenTripe.com
831-726-3255
www.greentripe.com

Halo, Purely for Pets
800-426-4256
www.halopets.com

Happy Dog Food
800-359-9576
www.happydogfood.com

Harbingers of a New Age
(entirely vegan)
406-295-4944
www.vegepet.com

Holistic Blend
800-954-1117
www.holisticblend.com

The Honest Kitchen
858-483-5995
www.thehonestkitchen.com

Know Better Dog Food
866-922-6463
www.knowbetterdogfood.com

KosherPets, Inc.
954-938-6270
www.kosherpets.com

Kumpi Pet Foods
303-699-8562
www.kumpi.com

Natural Balance Pet Foods, Inc.
(vegan options)
800-829-4493
www.naturalbalanceinc.com

Natural Life Pet Products, Inc.
(vegan options)
800-367-2391
www.nlpp.com

Nature's Variety
888-519-7387
www.naturesvariety.com

Newman's Own Organics
www.newmansownorganics.com

PetGuard
(vegan options)
800-874-3221
904-264-8500
www.petguard.com

Pied Piper Pet & Wildlife
800-338-4610
www.piedpiperpet.com

PoshNosh, Inc.
613-747-1542
866-893-4006
www.poshnosh.ca

Raw Advantage, Inc.
360-387-5158
www.rawadvantagepetfood.com

Rocky Mountain Natural Products
877-768-6788
(Eastern U.S.)
800-665-5521
(Western U.S.)
www.rmtnp.com

Sauder Feeds, Inc.
260-627-2196
www.sauderfeeds.com

Stella & Chewy's LLC
718-522-9673
www.stellaandchewys.com

Timberwolf Organics, Inc.
863-439-0049
www.timberwolforganics.com

Veterinary Nutritional Formula
800-811-0530
www.vnfpetfood.com

Wow-Bow Distributors Ltd.
(vegan options)
800-326-0230
www.wow-bow.com

Wysong Professional Diets
(vegan options)
800-748-0188
www.wysong.net

ANIMAL INGREDIENTS
& THEIR ALTERNATIVES

PETA's list of animal ingredients and their alternatives is designed to help you avoid animal ingredients in food, cosmetics, and other products. Please note, however, that it is not all-inclusive. There are thousands of technical and patented names for ingredient variations. Furthermore, some ingredients with the same name can be of animal, vegetable, or synthetic origin. **If you have a question regarding an ingredient in a product, please call the manufacturer directly.**

Good sources of additional information are *A Consumer's Dictionary of Cosmetic Ingredients, A Consumer's Dictionary of Food Additives*, or an unabridged dictionary. All these are available at most libraries.

Adding to the confusion about whether or not an ingredient is of animal origin is the fact that many companies have removed the word "animal" from their ingredient labels to avoid putting off consumers. For example, rather than using the term "hydrolyzed animal protein," companies may use another term such as "hydrolyzed collagen"—simple for them but frustrating for caring consumers.

Animal ingredients are used not because they are better than vegetable-derived or synthetic ingredients, but because they are generally cheaper. Today's slaughterhouses must dispose of the byproducts of the slaughter of billions of animals every year and have found an easy and profitable solution in selling them to food and cosmetics manufacturers.

Animal ingredients come from every industry that uses animals—the meat, fur, wool, dairy, egg, and fishing industries, as well as industries such as horse racing and rodeo, which send unwanted animals to slaughter. Contact PETA for factsheets or check out PETA.org to learn more about animals who suffer in these industries and what you can do to help stop it.

Rendering plants process millions of tons of dead animals every year, transforming decaying flesh and bones into profitable animal ingredients. The primary source of rendered animals is slaughterhouses, which provide the "inedible" parts of animals who were killed for food. The bodies of companion animals who are euthanized in animal shelters wind up at rendering plants, too. The city of Los Angeles sends 200 tons of euthanized cats and dogs to rendering plants every month, a sobering reminder of the horrible dog and cat overpopulation problem with which animal shelters must cope.

ANIMAL INGREDIENTS & THEIR ALTERNATIVES

Some animal ingredients do not wind up in the final product but are used in the manufacturing process. For example, in the production of some refined sugars, bone char is used to whiten the sugar and in some wines and beers, isinglass (from the swim bladders of fish) is used as a "clearing" agent.

Kosher symbols and markings also add to the confusion and are not reliable indicators on which vegans or vegetarians should base their purchasing decisions. This issue is complex, but the "K" or "Kosher" symbols basically mean that the food-manufacturing process was overseen by a rabbi, who ensured that it met Hebrew dietary laws. Kosher foods may not contain both dairy products and meat, but they may contain one or the other. "P" or "Pareve" symbols mean that the product contains no meat or dairy products but may contain fish or eggs. "D," as in "Kosher D," means that the product either contains dairy products or was made with dairy machinery. For example, a dark-chocolate candy may be marked "Kosher D" even if it doesn't contain dairy products because the nondairy chocolate was manufactured on machinery that also made milk chocolate. For questions regarding other symbols, please consult Jewish organizations or publications.

Thousands of products have labels that are hard to decipher. It's nearly impossible to be perfectly vegan, but it's getting easier to avoid products with animal ingredients. Our list will give you a good working knowledge of the most common animal-derived ingredients and their alternatives, allowing you to make decisions that will save animals' lives.

Adrenaline.
Hormone from adrenal glands of hogs, cattle, and sheep. In medicine. Alternatives *Synthetics*.

Alanine.
(See **Amino Acids**.)

Albumen.
In eggs, milk, muscles, blood, and many vegetable tissues and fluids. In cosmetics, albumen is usually derived from egg whites and used as a coagulating agent. May cause allergic reaction. In cakes, cookies, candies, etc. Egg whites sometimes used in "clearing" wines. Derivative **Albumin**.

Albumin.
(See **Albumen**.)

Alcloxa.
(See **Allantoin**.)

Aldioxa.
(See **Allantoin**.)

Aliphatic Alcohol.
(See **Lanolin** and **Vitamin A**.)

Allantoin.
Uric acid from cows and most mammals. Also in many plants (especially comfrey). In cosmetics (especially creams and lotions) and used in treatment of wounds and ulcers. Derivatives **Alcloxa**, **Aldioxa**. Alternatives *Extract of comfrey root, synthetics*.

Alligator Skin.
(See **Leather**.)

Alpha-Hydroxy Acids.
Any one of several acids used as an exfoliant and in anti-wrinkle products. Lactic acid may be animal-derived (see **Lactic Acid**). Alternatives *Glycolic acid, citric acid, and salicylic acid are plant- or fruit-derived*.

Ambergris.
From whale intestines. Used as a fixative in making perfumes and as a flavoring in foods and beverages. Alternatives *Synthetic or vegetable fixatives*.

Amino Acids.
The building blocks of protein in all animals and plants. In cosmetics, vitamins, supplements, shampoos, etc. Alternatives *Synthetics, plant sources*.

Aminosuccinate Acid.
(See **Aspartic Acid**.)

Amylase.
An enzyme from the pancreas of a pig. Used as a texturizer in cosmetics.

Angora.
Hair from the Angora rabbit or goat. Used in clothing. Alternatives *Synthetic fibers*.

Animal Fats and Oils.
In foods, cosmetics, etc. Highly allergenic. Alternatives *Olive oil, wheat germ oil, coconut oil, flaxseed oil, almond oil, safflower oil, etc.*

Animal Hair.
In some blankets, mattresses, brushes, furniture, etc. Alternatives *Vegetable and synthetic fibers*.

Arachidonic Acid.
A liquid unsaturated fatty acid found in the liver, brain, glands, and fat of animals and humans. Generally isolated from animal liver. Used in companion-animal food for nutrition and in skin creams and lotions to soothe eczema and rashes. Alternatives *Synthetics, aloe vera, tea tree oil, calendula ointment*.

Arachidyl Proprionate.
A wax that can be from animal fat. Alternatives *Peanut or vegetable oil*.

Aspartic Acid. Aminosuccinate Acid.
Can have animal or plant source (e.g., molasses). Sometimes synthesized for commercial purposes.

ANIMAL INGREDIENTS & THEIR ALTERNATIVES

Bee Pollen.
Microsporic grains in seed plants gathered by bees, then collected from the legs of bees. Causes allergic reactions in some people. In nutritional supplements, shampoos, toothpastes, and deodorants. Alternatives *Synthetics, plant amino acids, pollen collected from plants.*

Bee Products.
Produced by bees for their own use. Bees are selectively bred. Culled bees are killed. A cheap sugar is substituted for their stolen honey. Millions die as a result. Their legs are often torn off by pollen-collection trapdoors.

Beeswax. Honeycomb.
Wax obtained from melting honeycomb with boiling water, straining it, and cooling it. From virgin bees. Very cheap and widely used. May be harmful to the skin. In lipsticks and many other cosmetics (especially face creams, lotions, mascara, eye creams and shadows, face makeups, nail whiteners, lip balms, etc.). Derivatives **Cera Flava.** Alternatives *Paraffin, vegetable oils and fats, ceresin (also known as ceresine or earth wax; made from the mineral ozokerite; replaces beeswax in cosmetics; used to wax paper and to make polishing cloths, wax impressions in dentistry, and candles), carnauba wax (made from the Brazilian palm tree; used in many cosmetics, including lipstick; rarely causes allergic reactions), candelilla wax (from candelilla plants; used in many cosmetics, including lipstick; also used in the manufacture of rubber and phonography records, in waterproofing, and in ink; no known toxicity), Japan wax (also known as vegetable wax or Japan tallow, fat from the fruit of a tree grown in Japan and China).*

Benzoic Acid.
In almost all vertebrates and in berries. Used as a preservative in mouthwashes, deodorants, creams, aftershave lotions, etc. Alternatives *Cranberries, gum benzoin (tincture) from the aromatic balsamic resin from trees grown in China, Sumatra, Thailand, and Cambodia.*

Beta Carotene.
(See **Carotene.**)

Biotin. Vitamin H. Vitamin B Factor.
In every living cell and in larger amounts in milk and yeast. Used as a texturizer in cosmetics, shampoos, and creams. Alternatives *Plant sources.*

Blood.
From any slaughtered animal. Used as adhesive in plywood. Also found in foam rubber, intravenous feedings, and medicines. Possibly in foods such as lecithin. Alternatives *Synthetics, plant sources.*

Boar Bristles.
Hair from wild or captive hogs. In "natural" toothbrushes and bath and shaving brushes. Alternatives *Vegetable fibers, nylon, the peelu branch or peelu gum (Asian, available in the U.S.; its juice replaces toothpaste).*

Bone Char.
Animal bone ash. Used in bone china and often to whiten sugar. Serves as the charcoal used in aquarium filters. Alternatives *Synthetic tribasic calcium phosphate.*

Bone Meal.
Crushed or ground animal bones. In some fertilizers. In some vitamins and supplements as a source of calcium. In toothpastes. Alternatives *Plant mulch, vegetable compost, dolomite, clay, vegetarian vitamins.*

Calciferol.
(See **Vitamin D.**)

Calfskin.
(See **Leather.**)

Caprylamine Oxide.
(See **Caprylic Acid.**)

Capryl Betaine.
(See **Caprylic Acid.**)

Caprylic Acid.
A liquid fatty acid from cow's or goat's milk. Also from palm and coconut oil, other plant oils. In perfumes and soaps. Derivatives **Caprylic Triglyceride, Caprylamine Oxide, Capryl Betaine.** Alternatives *Plant sources.*

ANIMAL INGREDIENTS & THEIR ALTERNATIVES ▮

Caprylic Triglyceride.
(See **Caprylic Acid**.)

Carbamide.
(See **Urea**.)

Carmine. Cochineal. Carminic Acid.
Red pigment from the crushed female cochineal insect. Reportedly, 70,000 beetles must be killed to produce one pound of this red dye. Used in cosmetics, shampoos, red applesauce, and other foods (including red lollipops and food coloring). May cause allergic reaction. Alternatives *Beet juice (used in powders, rouges, and shampoos; no known toxicity), alkanet root (from the root of this herb-like tree; used as a red dye for inks, wines, lip balms, etc.; no known toxicity; can also be combined to make a copper or blue dye).* (See **Colors**.)

Carminic Acid.
(See **Carmine**.)

Carotene. Provitamin A. Beta Carotene.
A pigment found in many animal tissues and in all plants. Used as a coloring in cosmetics and in the manufacture of vitamin A.

Casein. Caseinate. Sodium Caseinate.
Milk protein. In "nondairy" creamers, soy cheese, many cosmetics, hair care products, and beauty masks. Alternatives *Soy protein, soy milk, and other vegetable milks.*

Caseinate.
(See **Casein**.)

Cashmere.
Wool from the Kashmir goat. Used in clothing. Alternatives *Synthetic fibers.*

Castor. Castoreum.
Creamy substance with strong odor from muskrat and beaver genitals. Used as a fixative in perfume and incense. Alternatives *Synthetics, plant castor oil.*

Castoreum.
(See **Castor**.)

Catgut.
Tough string from the intestines of sheep, horses, etc. Used for surgical sutures. Also for stringing tennis rackets, musical instruments, etc. Alternatives *Nylon and other synthetic fibers.*

Cera Flava.
(See **Beeswax**.)

Cerebrosides.
Fatty acids and sugars found in the covering of nerves. May include tissue from brains.

Cetyl Alcohol.
Wax found in spermaceti from sperm whales or dolphins. Alternatives *Vegetable cetyl alcohol (e.g., coconut), synthetic spermaceti.*

Cetyl Myristolete.
Produced by the reaction of cetyl alcohol and myristic acid (see both). Alternatives *Plant oils and synthetics.*

Cetyl Palmitate.
(See **Spermaceti**.)

Chitosan.
A fiber derived from crustacean shells. Used as a lipid binder in diet products, in hair, oral, and skin care products, antiperspirants, and deodorants. Alternatives *Raspberries, yams, legumes, dried apricots, and many other fruits and vegetables.*

Cholesterin.
(See **Lanolin**.)

Cholesterol.
A steroid alcohol in all animal fats and oils, nervous tissue, egg yolk, and blood. Can be derived from lanolin. In cosmetics, eye creams, shampoos, etc. Alternatives *Solid complex alcohols (sterols) from plant sources.*

Choline Bitartrate.
(See **Lecithin**.)

Chondroitin.
A common nutritional supplement. A major constituent of the cartilage of the body. Extracted from the cartilage of bovine

tracheas or shark cartilage. No known alternatives.

Civet.
Unctuous secretion painfully scraped from a gland very near the genital organs of civet cats. Used as a fixative in perfumes. Alternatives *(See alternatives to* **Musk***).*

Cochineal.
(See **Carmine**.)

Cod Liver Oil.
(See **Marine Oil**.)

Collagen.
Fibrous protein in vertebrates. Usually derived from animal tissue. Can't affect the skin's own collagen. An allergen. Alternatives *Soy protein, almond oil, amla oil (see alternatives to* **Keratin***), etc.*

Colors. Dyes.
Pigments from animal, plant, and synthetic sources used to color foods, cosmetics, and other products. Cochineal is from insects. Widely used FD&C and D&C colors are coal-tar (bituminous coal) derivatives that were tested on animals due to their carcinogenic properties. Alternatives *Grapes, beets, turmeric, saffron, carrots, chlorophyll, annatto, alkanet.*

Corticosteroid.
(See **Cortisone**.)

Cortisone. Corticosteroid.
Hormone from adrenal glands. Widely used in medicine. Alternatives *Synthetics.*

Cysteine, L-Form.
An amino acid from hair, often obtained from animals. Used in hair care products and creams, in some bakery products, and in wound-healing formulations.
Alternatives *Plant sources.*

Cystine.
An amino acid found in urine and horsehair. Used as a nutritional supplement and in emollients. Alternatives *Plant sources.*

Dexpanthenol.
(See **Panthenol**.)

Diglycerides.
(See **Monoglycerides** and **Glycerin**.)

Dimethyl Stearamine.
(See **Stearic Acid**.)

Docosahexanoic Acid (DHA).
Derived from fish oil. Commonly found in vitamins and supplements. Alternative *Flax seeds.*

Down.
Goose or duck insulating feathers. From slaughtered or cruelly exploited geese. Used as an insulator in quilts, parkas, sleeping bags, pillows, etc. Alternatives *Polyester and synthetic substitutes, kapok (silky fibers from the seeds of some tropical trees) and milkweed seed pod fibers.*

Duodenum Substances.
From the digestive tracts of cows and pigs. Added to some vitamin tablets. In some medicines. Alternatives *Vegetarian vitamins, synthetics.*

Dyes.
(See **Colors**.)

Egg Protein.
In shampoos, skin preparations, etc. Alternatives *Plant proteins.*

Eicosapentaenoic Acid.
Derived from fish oil. Commonly found in vitamins and supplements. Alternative *Flax seeds.*

Elastin.
Protein found in the neck ligaments and aortas of cows. Similar to collagen. Can't affect the skin's own elasticity. Alternatives *Synthetics, protein from plant tissues.*

Emu Oil. Kalaya Oil.
From flightless ratite birds native to Australia and now factory farmed. Used in cosmetics and creams. Alternatives *Vegetable and plant oils.*

Ergocalciferol.
(See **Vitamin D**.)

Ergosterol.
(See **Vitamin D**.)

Estradiol.
(See **Estrogen**.)

Estrogen. Estradiol.
Female hormones from pregnant mares' urine. Considered a drug. Can have harmful systemic effects if used by children. Used for reproductive problems and in birth control pills and Premarin, a menopausal drug. In creams, perfumes, and lotions. Has a negligible effect in the creams as a skin restorative; simple vegetable-source emollients are considered better. Alternatives *Oral contraceptives and menopausal drugs based on synthetic steroids or phytoestrogens (from plants, especially palm-kernel oil). Menopausal symptoms can also be treated with diet and herbs.*

Fats.
(See **Animal Fats**.)

Fatty Acids.
Can be one or any mixture of liquid and solid acids such as caprylic, lauric, myristic, oleic, palmitic, and stearic. Used in bubble baths, lipsticks, soap, detergents, cosmetics, and food. Alternatives *Vegetable-derived acids, soy lecithin, safflower oil, bitter almond oil, sunflower oil, etc.*

FD&C Colors.
(See **Colors**.)

Feathers.
From exploited and slaughtered birds. Used whole as ornaments or ground up in shampoos. (See **Down** and **Keratin**.)

Fish Liver Oil.
Used in vitamins and supplements. In milk fortified with vitamin D. Alternatives *Yeast extract ergosterol and exposure of skin to sunshine.*

Fish Oil.
(See **Marine Oil**.) Fish oil can also be from marine mammals. Used in soap-making.

Fish Scales.
Used in shimmery makeups. Alternatives *Mica, rayon, synthetic pearl.*

Fur.
Obtained from animals (usually minks, foxes, or rabbits) cruelly trapped in steel-jaw leghold traps or raised in intensive confinement on fur "farms." Alternatives *Synthetics.* (See **Sable Brushes**.)

Gelatin.
Protein obtained by boiling skin, tendons, ligaments, and/or bones with water. From cows and pigs. Used in shampoos, face masks, and other cosmetics. Used as a thickener for fruit gelatins and puddings (e.g., Jell-O®). In candies, marshmallows, cakes, ice cream, yogurts. On photographic film and in vitamins as a coating and as capsules. Sometimes used to assist in "clearing" wines. Alternatives *Carrageen (carrageenan, Irish moss), seaweeds (algin, agar-agar, kelp—used in jellies, plastics, medicine), pectin from fruits, dextrins, locust bean gum, cotton gum, silica gel. Marshmallows were originally made from the root of the marsh mallow plant. Vegetarian capsules are now available from several companies. Digital cameras don't use film.*

Glandular Extracts.
Extracts of animal glands are widely used in cosmetics. Alternatives *Plant extracts, synthetics.*

Glucosamine.
Derived from crustacean shells. Commonly found in vitamins and supplements.

Glucose Tyrosinase.
(See **Tyrosine**.)

Glycerides.
(See **Glycerin**.)

ANIMAL INGREDIENTS & THEIR ALTERNATIVES

Glycerin. Glycerol.
A byproduct of soap manufacture (normally uses animal fat). In cosmetics, foods, mouthwashes, chewing gum, toothpastes, soaps, ointments, medicines, lubricants, transmission and brake fluid, and plastics. Derivatives **Glycerides**, **Glyceryls**, **Glycreth-26**, **Polyglycerol**. Alternatives *Vegetable glycerin—a byproduct of vegetable oil soap, derivatives of seaweed, petroleum.*

Glycerol.
(See **Glycerin**.)

Glyceryls.
(See **Glycerin**.)

Glycreth-26.
(See **Glycerin**.)

Guanine. Pearl Essence.
Obtained from scales of fish. Constituent of ribonucleic acid and deoxyribonucleic acid. Found in all animal and plant tissues. In shampoo, nail polish, and other cosmetics. Alternatives *Leguminous plants, synthetic pearl, or aluminum and bronze particles.*

Hide Glue.
Same as gelatin but of a cruder, impure form. Alternatives *Dextrins and synthetic petrochemical-based adhesives.* (See **Gelatin**.)

Honey.
Food for bees, made by bees. Can cause allergic reactions. Used as a coloring and an emollient in cosmetics and as a flavoring in foods. Should never be fed to infants. Alternatives *In foods—maple syrup, date sugar, syrups made from grains such as barley malt, turbinado sugar, molasses; in cosmetics— vegetable colors and oils.*

Honeycomb.
(See **Beeswax**.)

Horsehair.
(See **Animal Hair**.)

Hyaluronic Acid.
A protein found in umbilical cords and the fluids around the joints. Used in cosmetics. Alternative *Synthetic hyaluronic acid, plant oils.*

Hydrocortisone.
(See **Cortisone**.)

Hydrolyzed Animal Protein.
In cosmetics, especially shampoo and hair treatments. Alternatives *Soy protein, other vegetable proteins, amla oil (see alternatives to* **Keratin***).*

Imidazolidinyl Urea.
(See **Urea**.)

Insulin.
From hog pancreas. Used by millions of diabetics daily. Alternatives *Synthetics, vegetarian diet and nutritional supplements, human insulin grown in a lab.*

Isinglass.
A form of gelatin prepared from the internal membranes of fish bladders. Sometimes used in "clearing" wines and in foods. Alternatives *Bentonite clay, "Japanese isinglass," agar-agar (see alternatives to* **Gelatin***), mica (a mineral used in cosmetics).*

Isopropyl Lanolate.
(See **Lanolin**.)

Isopropyl Myristate.
(See **Myristic Acid**.)

Isopropyl Palmitate.
Complex mixtures of isomers of stearic acid and palmitic acid. (See **Stearic Acid**.)

Kalaya Oil.
(See **Emu Oil**.)

Keratin.
Protein from the ground-up horns, hooves, feathers, quills, and hair of various animals. In hair rinses, shampoos, permanent wave solutions. Alternatives *Almond oil, soy protein, amla oil (from the fruit of an Indian tree), human hair from salons. Rosemary and nettle give body and strength to hair.*

Lactic Acid.
Found in blood and muscle tissue. Also in sour milk, beer, sauerkraut, pickles, and other food products made by bacterial fermentation. Used in skin fresheners, as a preservative, in the formation of plasticizers, etc. Alternatives *Plant milk sugars, synthetics.*

Lactose.
Milk sugar from the milk of mammals. In eye lotions, foods, tablets, cosmetics, baked goods, medicines. Alternative *Plant milk sugars.*

Laneth.
(See **Lanolin**.)

Lanogene.
(See **Lanolin**.)

Lanolin. Lanolin Acids. Wool Fat. Wool Wax.
A product of the oil glands of sheep, extracted from their wool. Used as an emollient in many skin care products and cosmetics and in medicines. An allergen with no proven effectiveness. (See **Wool** for cruelty to sheep information.) Derivatives **Aliphatic Alcohols, Cholesterin, Isopropyl Lanolate, Laneth, Lanogene, Lanolin Alcohols, Lanosterols, Sterols, Triterpene Alcohols.** Alternatives *Plant and vegetable oils.*

Lanolin Alcohol.
(See **Lanolin**.)

Lanosterols.
(See **Lanolin**.)

Lard.
Fat from hog abdomens. In shaving creams, soaps, and cosmetics. In baked goods, French fries, refried beans, and many other foods. Alternatives *Pure vegetable fats or oils.*

Leather. Suede. Calfskin. Sheepskin. Alligator Skin. Other Types of Skin.
Subsidizes the meat industry. Used to make wallets, handbags, furniture, car upholstery, shoes, etc. Alternatives *Cotton, canvas, nylon, vinyl, ultrasuede, pleather, other synthetics.*

Lecithin. Choline Bitartrate.
Waxy substance in the nervous tissue of all living organisms. Frequently obtained for commercial purposes from eggs and soybeans. Also from nerve tissue, blood, milk, and corn. Choline bitartrate, the basic constituent of lecithin, is in many animal and plant tissues and is also prepared synthetically. Lecithin can be in eye creams, lipsticks, liquid powders, hand creams, lotions, soaps, shampoos, other cosmetics, and some medicines. Alternatives *Soybean lecithin, synthetics.*

Linoleic Acid.
An essential fatty acid. Used in cosmetics and vitamins. Alternatives *(See alternatives to* **Fatty Acids***.)*

Lipase.
Enzyme from the stomachs and tongue glands of calves, kids, and lambs. Used in cheese-making and in digestive aids. Alternatives *Vegetable enzymes, castor beans.*

Lipids.
(See **Lipoids**.)

Lipoids. Lipids.
Fat and fat-like substances that are found in animals and plants. Alternative *Vegetable oils.*

Marine Oil.
From fish or marine mammals (including porpoises). Used in soap-making. Used as a shortening (especially in some margarines), as a lubricant, and in paint. Alternative *Vegetable oils.*

Methionine.
Essential amino acid found in various proteins (usually from egg albumen and casein). Used as a texturizer and for freshness in potato chips. Alternative *Synthetics.*

Milk Protein.
Hydrolyzed milk protein. From the milk of cows. In cosmetics, shampoos, moisturizers, conditioners, etc. Alternatives *Soy protein, other plant proteins.*

ANANTML INGREDIENTS & THEIR ALTERNATIVES

Mink Oil.
From minks. In cosmetics, creams, etc.
Alternatives *Vegetable oils and emollients such as avocado oil, almond oil, and jojoba oil.*

Monoglycerides. Glycerides.
(See **Glycerin**.) From animal fat. In margarines, cake mixes, candies, foods, etc. In cosmetics. Alternative *Vegetable glycerides.*

Musk (Oil).
Dried secretion painfully obtained from musk deer, beaver, muskrat, civet cat, and otter genitals. Wild cats are kept captive in cages in horrible conditions and are whipped around the genitals to produce the scent; beavers are trapped; deer are shot. In perfumes and in food flavorings. Alternatives *Labdanum oil (comes from various rockrose shrubs, has no known toxicity), other plants with musky scents.*

Myristal Ether Sulfate.
(See **Myristic Acid**.)

Myristic Acid.
Organic acid in most animal and vegetable fats. In butter acids. Used in shampoos, creams, and cosmetics. In food flavorings. Derivatives **Isopropyl Myristate**, **Myristal Ether Sulfate**, **Myristyls**, **Oleyl Myristate**. Alternatives *Nut butters, oil of lovage, coconut oil, extract from seed kernels of nutmeg, etc.*

Myristyls.
(See **Myristic Acid**.)

"Natural Sources."
Can mean animal or vegetable sources. Most often in the health food industry, especially in the cosmetics area, it means animal sources, such as animal elastin, glands, fat, protein, and oil. Alternatives *Plant sources.*

Nucleic Acids.
In the nucleus of all living cells. Used in cosmetics, shampoos, conditioners, etc. Also in vitamins and supplements. Alternatives *Plant sources.*

Ocenol.
(See **Oleyl Alcohol**.)

Octyl Dodecanol.
Mixture of solid waxy alcohols. Primarily from stearyl alcohol. (See **Stearyl Alcohol**.)

Oils.
(See alternatives to **Animal Fats and Oils**.)

Oleic Acid.
Obtained from various animal and vegetable fats and oils. Usually obtained commercially from inedible tallow. (See **Tallow**.) In foods, soft soap, bar soap, permanent wave solutions, creams, nail polish, lipsticks, many other skin preparations. Derivatives **Oleyl Oleate**, **Oleyl Stearate**. Alternatives *Coconut oil. (See alternatives to **Animal Fats and Oils**.)*

Oleths.
(See **Oleyl Alcohol**.)

Oleyl Alcohol. Ocenol.
Found in fish oils. Used in the manufacture of detergents, as a plasticizer for softening fabrics, and as a carrier for medications. Derivatives **Oleths**, **Oleyl Arachidate**, **Oleyl Imidazoline**.

Oleyl Arachidate.
(See **Oleyl Alcohol**.)

Oleyl Imidazoline.
(See **Oleyl Alcohol**.)

Oleyl Myristate.
(See **Myristic Acid**.)

Oleyl Oleate.
(See **Oleic Acid**.)

Oleyl Stearate.
(See **Oleic Acid**.)

Palmitamide.
(See **Palmitic Acid**.)

Palmitamine.
(See **Palmitic Acid**.)

Palmitate.
(See **Palmitic Acid**.)

Palmitic Acid.
From fats and oils (see **Fatty Acids**). Mixed with stearic acid. Found in many animal fats and plant oils. In shampoos, shaving soaps, and creams. Derivatives **Palmitate, Palmitamine, Palmitamide**. Alternatives Palm oil, vegetable sources.

Panthenol. Dexpanthenol. Vitamin B-Complex Factor. Provitamin B-5.
Can come from animal or plant sources or synthetics. In shampoos, supplements, emollients, etc. In foods. Derivative **Panthenyl**. Alternatives Synthetics, plants.

Panthenyl.
(See **Panthenol**.)

Pepsin.
In hogs' stomachs. A clotting agent. In some cheeses and vitamins. Same uses and alternatives as **Rennet**.

Placenta. Placenta Polypeptides Protein. Afterbirth.
Contains waste matter eliminated by the fetus. Derived from the uterus of slaughtered animals. Animal placenta is widely used in skin creams, shampoos, masks, etc. Alternatives Kelp. (See alternatives to **Animal Fats and Oils**.)

Polyglycerol.
(See **Glycerin**.)

Polypeptides.
From animal protein. Used in cosmetics. Alternatives Plant proteins and enzymes.

Polysorbates.
Derivatives of fatty acids. In cosmetics and foods.

Pristane.
Obtained from the liver oil of sharks and from whale ambergris. (See **Squalene, Ambergris**.) Used as a lubricant and anti-corrosive agent. In cosmetics. Alternatives Plant oils, synthetics.

Progesterone.
A steroid hormone used in anti-wrinkle face creams. Can have adverse systemic effects. Alternatives Synthetics.

Propolis.
Tree sap gathered by bees and used as a sealant in beehives. In toothpaste, shampoo, deodorant, supplements, etc. Alternatives Tree sap, synthetics.

Provitamin A.
(See **Carotene**.)

Provitamin B-5.
(See **Panthenol**.)

Provitamin D-2.
(See **Vitamin D**.)

Rennet. Rennin.
Enzyme from calves' stomachs. Used in cheese-making, rennet custard (junket), and many coagulated dairy products. Alternatives Microbial coagulating agents, bacteria culture, lemon juice, or vegetable rennet.

Rennin.
(See **Rennet**.)

Resinous Glaze.
(See **Shellac**.)

Ribonucleic Acid.
(See **RNA**.)

RNA. Ribonucleic Acid.
RNA is in all living cells. Used in many protein shampoos and cosmetics. Alternatives Plant cells.

ANIMAL INGREDIENTS & THEIR ALTERNATIVES ▬

Royal Jelly.
Secretion from the throat glands of the honeybee workers. Fed to the larvae in a colony and to all queen larvae. No proven value in cosmetics preparations. Alternatives *Aloe vera, comfrey, other plant derivatives.*

Sable Brushes.
From the fur of sables (weasel-like mammals). Used to make eye makeup, lipstick, and artists' brushes. Alternatives *Synthetic fibers.*

Sea Turtle Oil.
(See **Turtle Oil.**)

Shark Cartilage.
A common nutritional supplement. No known alternatives.

Shark Liver Oil.
Used in lubricating creams and lotions. Derivatives **Squalane, Squalene.** Alternatives *Vegetable oils.*

Sheepskin.
(See **Leather.**)

Shellac. Resinous Glaze.
Resinous excretion of certain insects. Used as a candy glaze, in hair lacquer, and on jewelry. Alternatives *Plant waxes.*

Silk. Silk Powder.
The shiny fiber made by silkworms to form their cocoons. Worms are boiled in their cocoons to get the silk. Used in cloth. In silk-screening (other fine cloth can be and is used instead). Taffeta can be made from silk or nylon. Silk powder is obtained from the secretion of the silkworm. Used as a coloring agent in face powders, soaps, etc. Can cause severe allergic skin reactions and systemic reactions (if inhaled or ingested). Alternatives *Milkweed seed-pod fibers, nylon, silk-cotton tree and ceiba tree filaments (kapok), rayon, synthetic silks.*

Snails.
In some cosmetics (crushed).

Sodium Caseinate.
(See **Casein.**)

Sodium Steroyl Lactylate.
(See **Lactic Acid.**)

Sodium Tallowate.
(See **Tallow.**)

Spermaceti. Cetyl Palmitate. Sperm Oil.
Waxy oil derived from the sperm whale's head or from dolphins. In many margarines. In skin creams, ointments, shampoos, candles, etc. Used in the leather industry. May become rancid and cause irritations. Alternatives *Synthetic spermaceti, jojoba oil, other vegetable emollients.*

Sponge (Luna and Sea).
A plant-like sea animal. Becoming scarce. Alternatives *Synthetic sponges, loofahs (plants used as sponges).*

Squalane.
(See **Shark Liver Oil.**)

Squalene.
Oil from shark livers, etc. In cosmetics, moisturizers, hair dyes, and surface-active agents. Alternatives *Vegetable emollients such as olive oil, wheat germ oil, rice bran oil, etc.*

Stearamide.
(See **Stearic Acid.**)

Stearamine.
(See **Stearic Acid.**)

Stearamine Oxide.
(See **Stearyl Alcohol.**)

Stearates.
(See **Stearic Acid.**)

Stearic Acid.
Fat from cows and sheep and from dogs and cats euthanized in animal shelters, etc. Most often refers to a fatty substance taken from the stomachs of pigs. Can be harsh, irritating. Used in cosmetics, soaps, lubricants, candles, hairspray, conditioners, deodorants, creams, chewing gum, and food flavoring. Derivatives **Stearamide, Stearamine, Stearates, Stearic Hydrazide, Stearone, Stearoxytrimethylsilane, Stearoyl Lactylic Acid, Stearyl Betaine, Stearyl Imidazoline.** Alternatives *Stearic acid can be found in many vegetable fats and in coconut.*

Stearic Hydrazide.
(See **Stearic Acid.**)

Stearone.
(See **Stearic Acid.**)

Stearoxytrimethylsilane.
(See **Stearic Acid.**)

Stearoyl Lactylic Acid.
(See **Stearic Acid.**)

Stearyl Acetate.
(See **Stearyl Alcohol.**)

Stearyl Alcohol. Sterols.
A mixture of solid alcohols. Can be prepared from sperm whale oil. In medicines, creams, rinses, shampoos, etc. Derivatives **Stearamine Oxide, Stearyl Acetate, Stearyl Caprylate, Stearyl Citrate, Stearyldimethyl Amine, Stearyl Glycyrrhetinate, Stearyl Heptanoate, Stearyl Octanoate, Stearyl Stearate.** Alternatives *Plant sources, vegetable stearic acid.*

Stearyl Betaine.
(See **Stearic Acid.**)

Stearyl Caprylate.
(See **Stearyl Alcohol.**)

Stearyl Citrate.
(See **Stearyl Alcohol.**)

Stearyldimethyl Amine.
(See **Stearyl Alcohol.**)

Stearyl Glycyrrhetinate.
(See **Stearyl Alcohol.**)

Stearyl Heptanoate.
(See **Stearyl Alcohol.**)

Stearyl Imidazoline.
(See **Stearic Acid.**)

Stearyl Octanoate.
(See **Stearyl Alcohol.**)

Stearyl Stearate.
(See **Stearyl Alcohol.**)

Steroids. Sterols.
From various animal glands or from plant tissues. Steroids include sterols. Sterols are alcohol from animals or plants (e.g., cholesterol). Used in hormone preparation. In creams, lotions, hair conditioners, fragrances, etc. Alternatives *Plant tissues, synthetics.*

Sterols.
(See **Stearyl Alcohol** and **Steroids.**)

Suede.
(See **Leather.**)

Tallow. Tallow Fatty Alcohol.
Stearic Acid.
Rendered beef fat. May cause eczema and blackheads. In wax paper, crayons, margarines, paints, rubber, lubricants, etc. In candles, soaps, lipsticks, shaving creams, and other cosmetics. Chemicals (e.g., PCB) can be in animal tallow. Derivatives **Sodium Tallowate, Tallow Acid, Tallow Amide, Tallow Amine, Talloweth-6, Tallow Glycerides, Tallow Imidazoline.** Alternatives *Vegetable tallow, Japan tallow, paraffin, and/or ceresin (see alternatives to **Beeswax** for all three). Paraffin is usually from petroleum, wood, coal, or shale oil.*

Tallow Acid.
(See **Tallow.**)

Tallow Amide.
(See **Tallow**.)

Tallow Amine.
(See **Tallow**.)

Talloweth-6.
(See **Tallow**.)

Tallow Glycerides.
(See **Tallow**.)

Tallow Imidazoline.
(See **Tallow**.)

Triterpene Alcohols.
(See **Lanolin**.)

Turtle Oil. Sea Turtle Oil.
From the muscles and genitals of giant sea turtles. In soap, skin creams, nail creams, and other cosmetics. Alternatives *Vegetable emollients (see alternatives to* **Animal Fats and Oils***).*

Tyrosine.
Amino acid hydrolyzed from casein. Used in cosmetics and creams. Derivative **Glucose Tyrosinase**.

Urea. Carbamide.
Excreted from urine and other bodily fluids. In deodorants, ammoniated dentifrices, mouthwashes, hair color, hand creams, lotions, shampoos, etc. Used to "brown" baked goods, such as pretzels. Derivatives **Imidazolidinyl Urea**, **Uric Acid**. Alternatives *Synthetics.*

Uric Acid.
(See **Urea**.)

Vitamin A.
Can come from fish liver oil (e.g., shark liver oil), egg yolk, butter, lemongrass, wheat germ oil, carotene in carrots, and synthetics. It is an aliphatic alcohol. In cosmetics, creams, perfumes, hair dyes, etc. In vitamins and supplements. Alternatives *Carrots, other vegetables, synthetics.*

Vitamin B-Complex Factor.
(See **Panthenol**.)

Vitamin B Factor.
(See **Biotin**.)

Vitamin B-12.
Can come from animal products or bacteria cultures. Twinlab B-12 vitamins contain gelatin. Alternatives *Vegetarian vitamins, fortified soy milks, fortified meat substitutes, and nutritional yeast. Vitamin B12 is often listed as "cyanocobalamin" on food labels. Vegan health professionals caution that vegans should get 5 to 10 mcg/day of vitamin B12 from fortified foods or supplements.*

Vitamin D. Ergocalciferol. Vitamin D-2. Ergosterol. Provitamin D-2. Calciferol. Vitamin D-3.
Vitamin D can come from fish liver oil, milk, egg yolk, etc. Vitamin D-2 can come from animal fats or plant sterols. Vitamin D-3 is always from an animal source. All the D vitamins can be in creams, lotions, other cosmetics, vitamin tablets, etc. Alternatives *Plant and mineral sources, synthetics, vegan vitamins, exposure of skin to sunshine. Many other vitamins can come from animal sources. Examples: choline, biotin, inositol, riboflavin, etc.*

Vitamin H.
(See **Biotin**.)

Wax.
Glossy, hard substance that is soft when hot. From animals and plants. In lipsticks, depilatories, hair straighteners. Alternatives *Vegetable waxes.*

Whey.
A serum from milk. Usually in cakes, cookies, candies, and breads. Used in cheese-making. Alternative *Soybean whey.*

ANIMAL INGREDIENTS & THEIR ALTERNATIVES

REFERENCES

* Buyukmihci, Nermin. "John Cardillo's List of Animal Products and Their Alternatives."
* *Cosmetic Ingredients Glossary: A Basic Guide to Natural Body Care Products.* Petaluma, Calif.: Feather River Co., 1988.
* Mason, Jim, and Peter Singer. *Animal Factories.* New York: Crown Publishers, Inc., 1980.
* Ruesch, Hans. *Slaughter of the Innocent.* New York: Civitas, 1983.
* Singer, Peter. *Animal Liberation.* New York: Random House, 1990.
* Sweethardt Herb Catalogue.
* *Webster's Third New International Dictionary.* Springfield, Mass.: Merriam-Webster Inc., 1981.
* Winter, Ruth. *A Consumer's Dictionary of Cosmetic Ingredients.* New York: Crown Publishing Group, 1994.
* Winter, Ruth. *A Consumer's Dictionary of Food Additives.* New York: Crown Publishing Group, 1994.

ALTERNATIVES TO LEATHER
& OTHER ANIMAL PRODUCTS ▬▬▬▬▬

What's Wrong With Leather?

■ Millions of cows, pigs, sheep, and goats are slaughtered for their skin every year. They are castrated, branded, and dehorned and have thier tails cut off without anesthetics. Then they are trucked to slaughter, bled to death, and skinned.

■ Leather is not simply a slaughterhouse byproduct. The meat industry relies on skin sales to stay in business because the skin represents the most economically important byproduct of the meat industry, according to the U.S. Department of Agriculture.

■ Animal skin is turned into leather through the use of dangerous mineral salts, formaldehyde, coal-tar derivatives, cyanide-based oils and dyes, and other toxins.

■ People who have worked in and lived near tanneries are dying of cancer caused by exposure to toxic chemicals used to process and dye the leather. A New York State Department of Health study found that more than half of all testicular cancer victims in the U.S. work in tanneries.

■ When you buy leather products, you may be purchasing leather from Asian dog and cat tanneries; since product labeling rarely indicates where the skins originate, there's no way to know for sure.

Visit **CowsAreCool.com** for more information on the leather industry.

What's Wrong With Wool?

■ Sheep need the wool that they produce to protect themselves from temperature extremes.

ALTERNATIVES TO LEATHER
& OTHER ANIMAL PRODUCTS

■ Shearing sheep involves more than just a haircut. Because shearers are usually paid by volume rather than by the hour, they often work too fast and disregard the animals' welfare. Sheep are routinely punched, kicked, and cut during the shearing process.

■ Much of the world's wool comes from Australia and New Zealand, where almost 140 million sheep each year undergo a gruesome procedure called "mulesing," in which gardening/huge shears are used to slice chunks of skin and flesh off the backsides of live animals without anesthetics.

■ Millions of sheep raised for wool in Australia and New Zealand are shipped to the Middle East for slaughter. These animals are placed on extremely crowded ships with little access to food or water for weeks or even months. During their grueling journeys, they suffer through weather extremes, and temperatures on the ships can exceed 100°F. Many fall ill when they become stuck in feces and are unable to move, and many others are smothered or trampled to death by other sheep.

■ Intense sheep farming, especially in Australia, is responsible for the degradation of natural waterways and land habitats and for the emission of greenhouse gases, such as methane, into the atmosphere.

■ When you buy wool products, it is likely that you are buying wool from sheep who were raised in Australia or New Zealand no matter what the label says, since most wool is routed through China or Italy for processing, and product labeling rarely indicates where it originated. However, sheep farming involves cruelty regardless of the country in which the animals are raised.

Visit **SavetheSheep.com** for more information on the wool industry.

What's Wrong With Silk?

■ Silk is the fiber that silkworms weave to make cocoons. To obtain silk, manufacturers boil worms alive in their cocoons. Humane alternatives to silk include nylon, milkweed seed-pod fibers, silk-cotton tree and ceiba tree filaments, and rayon.

What's Wrong With Down?

■ Down, which is used to fill comforters, pillows, ski parkas, and other products, is the soft underfeathering of geese.

■ Geese are plucked of their down either after slaughter or while being raised for meat or *foie gras* (i.e., "fatty liver," produced by force-feeding geese through a pipe jammed down thier throats until their livers balloon to seven to 12 times their normal size).

■ Plucking birds causes them considerable pain and distress; one study found that the blood glucose level of geese nearly doubled as they were being plucked.

■ Down is expensive and loses its insulating ability when wet, while the insulating capabilities of cruelty-free synthetic fillers persist in all weather.

Shopping Tips

Whether you're trying on pleather pumps at Payless or digging through Nordstrom's racks for faux shearling, synthetic alternatives are easy to find and are often clearly labeled. Forget about out-of-the-way specialty shops. From discount department stores like Target and TJ Maxx to hip boutiques like Diesel and Paul Frank and everything in between (think Linens 'n Things, JCPenney, or even Victoria's Secret), mainstream stores have become meccas for compassionate shoppers.

Here are some general tips. If you're shopping for alternatives to …

■ Leather

Look under shoe tongues, on tags, and on the insides of belts and bags for fake-leather buzzwords like "manmade leather," "all-manmade materials," "pleather," and "synthetic." No label or unsure? Ask a salesperson if it is "real" leather. Finally, the price may clue you in. Typically, fake leather sells at a fraction of the price of animal leather!

ALTERNATIVES TO LEATHER
& OTHER ANIMAL PRODUCTS

Hint: You'll find a continually changing stock of synthetic shoes if you drop into shoe warehouses and designer discount stores such as Off Broadway, Parade of Shoes, DSW, and Marshalls. It is just as easy to steer clear of skins at upscale department stores like Macy's and Saks Fifth Avenue, with most trendy and high-end lines, including Chinese Laundry, Kenneth Cole, Nine West, and Kate Spade, featuring pleather footwear and accessories.

■ Wool, Cashmere, Mohair, etc.

Watch out for wool hiding in pants and suits (read labels!), and take a pass on pashmina, angora, cashmere, shearling, camel hair, and mohair, too—all made from animals. Instead, look for snuggly warm synthetic fabrics, such as polyester fleece, acrylic, and cotton flannel—they wash easily, keep their bright colors, cost less, and don't contribute to cruelty.

Heavy, bulky wool can't hold a candle to revolutionary new fabrics like Gore-Tex, Thermolite, Thinsulate, and Polartec Wind Pro, which is made primarily from recycled plastic soda bottles and has four times the wind resistance of wool. It also wicks away moisture and is available at Patagonia and other outdoor outfitters.

Tencel, a natural fabric made from wood pulp, is a breathable, durable, and biodegradable alternative to wool for men's and women's dress suits. If you're looking for a suit, start shopping in the spring, when summer suits made from cotton, viscose, and other lighter materials are available from retailers such as 99X, TravelSmith, Pangea, and others.

For nonwool tuxedos, try ETuxedo.com or CheapTux.com.

■ Silk

Find humane alternatives to silk ties and other silk items—such as nylon, polyester, rayon, Tencel, milkweed seed pod fibers, and even silk-cotton tree and ceiba tree filaments—online and in stores for a fraction of the price of silk. Cruelty-free Ahimsa silk (ahimsapeacesilk.com or www.organicavenue.com), produced in India for Hindus by the company Designer Weaves, is made from the cocoons of caterpillars who have completed the moth stage and flown away.

■ Down

Down-free coats, sleeping bags, comforters, pillows, and more can be found virtually anywhere, including Eddie Bauer, The Company Store, and Bed Bath & Beyond. Look for labels that say "synthetic down," "down alternative," or "polyester fill," or buy high-tech fabrics like Primaloft, a soft, washable, downlike fiber that is often used in coats, gloves, and comforters—unlike down, it even stays warm when it's wet.

■ Fur

Coats with fur collars and trim and fur accessories hurt animals too. Just read labels to weed out cruel products. Cruelty-free faux furs made of plush modern synthetics are becoming so easy to find. Fabulous Furs sells elegant, stylish coats that are completely faux. Many other designers and manufacturers, including Charly Calder, Faux, Purrfect Fur, and Sweet Herb, are specializing in fabulous faux furs as well.

Visit **FurIsDead.com** for more information on the fur industry.

Buying animal-free shoes, belts, wallets, bags, sweaters, and jackets has never been easier. This section is divided into three parts: companies that sell only vegan products, companies that sell some leather and fur alternatives, and an easy-to-use list of companies organized by type of product.

Visit **CaringConsumer.com** for the most up-to-date company information.

🛒 Company's products can be purchased through PETA at PETAMall.com. PETA will receive 5 to 20 percent of every purchase at no extra cost to you. Please see company listings on PETAMall.com for exact percentages.

ALTERNATIVES TO LEATHER
& OTHER ANIMAL PRODUCTS

All Vegan
619-299-4669
lca_sandiego@bigfoot.com
www.alternativeoutfitters.com
Sells locally in San Diego, Calif.: vegan shoes, belts, and purses.

Alternative Outfitters
626-396-4972
customercare@alternativeoutfitters.com
www.alternativeoutfitters.com
Nonleather women's shoes, handbags, wallets, belts, watches, cell phone pouches, and other accessories.

Bagg Lady Handbags
800-459-3033
info@bagglady.com
www.bagglady.com
Versatile synthetic leather purses designed with a built-in wallet for maximum space, efficiency, accessibility, and organization.

Beyond Skin
011 44 0207 1494 871655
info@beyondskin.co.uk
www.beyondskin.co.uk
Vegan shoes for women.

Bootzwalla
917-905-3313
ori@bootzwalla.com
www.bootzwalla.com
Imported faux fur hats, scarves, and leggings.

Bulge
800-630-9389
sales@bulgebag.com
www.bulgebag.com
Hip bags made from a water-resistant PVC material.

Cedar Key Canvas
800-729-0297
julie@ckcanvas.com
www.ckcanvas.com
Handcrafted and custom-made canvas totes, purses, luggage, and duffels.

Chrome Bags
415-503-1221
chrome@chromebags.com
www.chromebags.com
Nonleather messenger bags, laptop bags, and DJ bags.

Comfurts by Ken Alan
323-951-0045
kalan@comfurts.com
www.comfurts.com
Faux fur pillows, throws, home furnishings, and robes.

Coquette Faux Furriers
claire@coquettefauxfurriers.com
www.coquettefauxfurriers.com
Faux fur hats, muffs, purses, collars, and stoles.

Crocs
303-998-6068
contact@crocs.com
www.crocs.com
Vegan slip-resistant footwear.

Crystalyn Kae
866-310-9377
info@crystalynkae.com
www.crystalynkae.com
Stylish vegan bags and belts.

Cynthia King Dance
718-437-0101
www.cynthiakingdance.com
Cynthiakingdance@aol.com
Nonleather ballet shoes.

Ductbill
503-263-6632
info@ductbills.com
www.ductbills.com
Vegan wallets.

Ethical Wares
011 44 15 7047 1155
vegans@ethicalwares.com
www.ethicalwares.com
Trekking and hiking boots, dress boots, steel-toed safety boots, belts, and dress shoes for men and women.
🛒

Faux
011 44 20 7253 5768
sales@faux.uk.co
www.faux.uk.com
Faux fur jackets, cushions, bedspreads, rugs, throws, handbags, scarves, bikinis, and accessories.

Freerangers
011 44 12 0756 5957
info@freerangers.co.uk
www.freerangers.co.uk
Vegan shoes, bags, belts, accessories, and clothing for men, women, and children.

Fur Replicas
888-756-7531
www.furreplicas.com
Faux fur jackets, capes, wraps, and muffs for rent or sale.

Gloria Gerber
330-867-2102
gloria@gloriagerber.com
www.gloriagerber.com
Vegan bags.

GoodGoth.com
413-568-6641
luluwhite@aol.com
www.goodgoth.com
Funky vinyl shoes, boots, bags, coats, skirts, dresses, and lingerie.

Heartland Products, Ltd.
800-441-4692 (U.S.)
515-332-3087 (Canada)
www.trvnet.net/~hrtlndp/
Nonleather Western-style boots, work boots, baseball gloves, shoes, watchbands, belts, and biker jackets.

Helen Powers
212-288-9847
helenpowersfit@aol.com
www.helenpowers.com
Vegan "Powerbag" versatile enough for the gym or traveling.

INOPIA Footwear
888-269-5366
info@inopiausa.com
www.inopiausa.com
Vegan belts, wallets, and BMX/skateboarding shoes.

Këpur
213-687-9699
info@kepur.com
www.kepur.com
Vegan guitar straps.

Little Packrats
978-449-0222
info@littlepackrats.com
www.littlepackrats.com
Fun vinyl backpacks, lunch bags, and totes for kids.

M. Avery Designs Studio & Boutique
201-876-1198
funkybags@maverydesigns.com
www.maverydesigns.com
Stylish nonleather bags.

Moo Shoes
212-481-5792
info@mooshoes.com
www.mooshoes.com
Wide variety of nonleather shoes, belts, and wallets.
🛒

N/A Designs
natalie@nadesigns.com
www.nadesigns.com
Vinyl bags and bracelets.

Nedra Made It
503-528-5284
www.nedramadeit.com
Vegan dog-gear bag and collapsible travel bowl.

ALTERNATIVES TO LEATHER
& OTHER ANIMAL PRODUCTS

NoBull Footwear
011 44 12 7330 2979
information@veganstore.co.uk
www.veganstore.co.uk
Vegan dress and casual shoes, hiking boots,
jackets, belts, and wallets.

OTSU
866-HEY-OTSU
info@veganmart.com
www.veganmart.com
Vegan shoes, belts, wallets, and bags.

Pangea
800-340-1200
info@veganstore.com
www.veganstore.com
Vegan shoes, belts, bags, boots, wallets, guitar
straps, jackets, ties, suits, and more.
🛒

Posh Pelts
customerservice@poshpelts.com
www.poshpelts.com
Faux fur pillows and throws.

Premium Furs
866-632-2387
contact@prefurs.com
www.prefurs.com
Faux fur fabrics, throws, pillows, and
lampshades.

Queen Bee Creations
503-232-1755
queenbee@queenbee-creations.com
www.queenbee-creations.com
Unique vinyl bags, wallets, and accessories,
custom-made to your specifications.

R.E. Load Baggage Inc.
East Coast: 215-922-2018
West Coast: 206-323-3281
info@reloadbags.com
www.reloadbags.com
Nonleather, custom-designed messenger bags.

Shoes With Souls
858-653-3741
info@shoeswithsouls.com
www.shoeswithsouls.com
Stylish vegan shoes and belts.

Slim Pawn Handmade Handbags
info@slimpawn.com
www.slimpawn.com
Handmade vegan bags.

Sparkle Craft
tina@sparklecraft.com
www.sparklecraft.com
Vegan guitar straps, belts, bags, and
accessories.

Splaff Flops
619-221-9199
www.splaff.com
Nonleather sandals, bags, and belts made
from recycled materials.

Stella McCartney
212-741-0141
sales@stellamccartney.com
www.stellamccartney.com
Nonleather accessories, bags, shoes, and
clothing.

Timbuk2 Designs
888-TIMBUK2
customerservice@timbuk2.com
www.timbuk2.com
Nonleather, custom-designed messenger and
computer bags.

Tom Bihn
800-729-9607
inquiries@tombihn.com
www.tombihn.com
Variety of nonleather bags, including laptop
cases, briefcases, messenger bags, travels, and
totes.
🛒

Truth
416-777-1604
truth@rogers.com
www.truthbelts.com
Fashionable nonleather belts and purses.

Used Rubber USA
415-626-7855
questions@usedrubberusa.com
www.usedrubberusa.com
Wallets, organizers, and bags made from
recycled rubber.

VeganErotica.com
801-560-8238
eward@veganerotica.com
www.veganerotica.com
Vegan condoms, bondage gear, and other
items.

Vegan Essentials
866-88-VEGAN
questions@veganessentials.com
www.veganessentials.com
Hemp shoes and clothing, nonleather shoes,
bags, belts, and wallets.

Veganline
nude@animal.nu
www.animal.nu
Stylish vegan shoes, boots, and belts.

Vegan Wares
011 44 12 7369 1913
veganw@veganwares.com
www.veganwares.com
Nonleather shoes, belts, boots, briefcases,
wallets, guitar straps, dog collars, jazz shoes,
and ballet slippers.

Vegetarian Shoes
011 44 12 7369 1913
information@vegetarian-shoes.co.uk
www.vegetarian-shoes.co.uk
Pleather jackets and belts and more than 50
styles of synthetic leather and synthetic suede
shoes, including Birkenstocks, dress shoes,
hiking boots, and work boots.

TheVegetarianSite.com
520-529-8691
shopping@thevegetariansite.com
www.thevegetariansite.com
Vegan shoes, bags, wallets, and accessories.

Via Vegan
888-304-2334
info@viavegan.com
www.viavegan.com
Stylish nonleather purses and wallets.

Vulcana Bags
info@vulcanabags.com
www.vulcanabags.com
Wallets, organizers, and bags made from
recycled rubber.

OTHER COMPANIES THAT SELL LEATHER ALTERNATIVES
To find out where the following companies'
products can be purchased, please contact
them directly.

Active Soles
800-881-4322
sales@activesoles.com
www.activesoles.com
Several styles of synthetic New Balance shoes
for men and women.

Adidas
800-982-9337
customerservice@thestore.adidas.com
www.adidas.com
Many styles of nonleather athletic shoes,
including football, baseball, and soccer cleats.

Aerosoles
800-798-9478
catalog@aerosoles.com
www.aerosoles.com
Some styles of casual and dress shoes
available in synthetic leather.

Aerostich/Rider Warehouse
800-222-1994
products@aerostich.com
www.aerostich.com
Nonleather cycling apparel.

Airwalk
www.airwalk.com
Synthetic snowboarding boots.

ALTERNATIVES TO LEATHER
& OTHER ANIMAL PRODUCTS

Alloy
888-45-ALLOY
cs@alloy.com
www.alloy.com
Good selection of nonleather shoes.

Alpine Stars
800-438-2577
talk-to-us@alpinestars.com
www.alpinestars.com
Nonleather motorcycle jackets, gloves, and
pants.

American Tigerstrike, Inc
951-520-002
martialartsorders@earthlink.net
Vegan half finger punching gloves.

Anywear Shoes
888-425-0077
info@anywears.com
www.anywears.com
Brightly colored, biodegradable padded clogs.

Á Propos … Conversations
800-SHOES-2-GO
sales@conversationshoes.com
www.conversationshoes.com
Nonleather shoes for women.

Asics
800-678-9435
consumer@asicstiger.com
www.asicstiger.com
Synthetic athletic shoes.

Avia
888-855-2842
service@avia.com
www.avia.com
Synthetic athletic shoes.

Bakers Shoe Store
877-SHOEWEB
service@bakersshoes.com
www.bakersshoes.com
Nonleather shoes for women.

Bata Shoe Company, Inc.
416-446-2011
batalim@toronto.bata.com
www.bata.com
Industrial footwear and protective clothing:
nonleather high- and low-top boots suitable
for factory or farm work.

Birkenstock Footwear
800-824-1228
info@birkenstock.com
www.birkenstock.com
Several styles of nonleather clogs and sandals.

Burlington Coat Factory
www.burlingtoncoatfactory.com
Nonleather dress and casual shoes and some
faux fur coats.

Burton Snowboards
800-881-3138
info@burton.com
www.burton.com
Several styles of synthetic snowboarding
boots.

Capezio
800-234-4858
dmattews@balletmakers.com
www.capeziodance.com
Synthetic tap and dance shoes (styles include
"ZooTechnique," which is available by special
order and the "Jr. Tyette").

Charlotte Russe
877-266-9327
charlotte@charlotte-russe.com
www.charlotte-russe.com
Some faux fur and nonleather bags, shoes,
jackets, and boots.

Charly Calder International
415-215-1108
info@charly.cc
www.charlycalder.com
Faux fur coats.

Chinese Laundry Shoes
310-838-2103
www.chineselaundry.com
Fashionable women's shoes made with linen, microfiber, and other synthetic materials.

Circa
www.circafootwear.com
Nonleather skateboarding shoes (Jamie Thomas Pro Series).

Cloudwalkers
800-752-1330
www.cloudwalkers.com
Comfortable shoes available in wide widths.

Coldwater Creek
800-510-2808
www.coldwatercreek.com
Nonleather boots and dress shoes.

Coldwave Snowmobile Apparel
616-866-3722
coldwavecustserv@ssltd.org
www.coldwavesnowwear.com
Nonleather snowmobile apparel.

Competition Accessories
800-543-5141
custservice@compacc.com
www.competitionaccessories.com
Nonleather cycling apparel.

Converse
800-428-2667 (U.S.)
800-387-9550 (Canada)
www.converse.com
"Chuck Taylor All-Stars," high-top and low-top, in many styles, colors, and fabrics.

Delia's
212-807-9060
espeak@delias.com or custserv@delias.com
www.delias.com
Hip clothes and a good selection of nonleather shoes.

Dennis Kirk
800-328-9280
info@denniskirk.com
www.denniskirk.com
Nonleather cycling apparel.

Dexter Shoes
888-8-DEXTER
www.dextershoe.com
Several synthetic styles of men's and women's bowling shoes and golf cleats.

Diesel
212-755-9200
www.diesel.com
Some synthetic shoes and bags.

Dillard's
501-376-5200
www.dillards.com
Faux fur and shearling coats.

DiMarzio, Inc.
800-221-6468
on-line@dimarzio.com
www.dimarzio.com
Nonleather guitar straps.

Dragonfly
800-995-4848
info@dragonflyshoes.com
www.dragonflyshoes.com
Nonleather shoes, boots, and bags.

DSW
800-477-8595
www.dswshoe.com
Nonleather shoes and bags.

Earth
877-372-2814
www.earth.us
Nonleather shoes.

Ecolution
800-973-HEMP
sales@ecolution.com
www.ecolution.com
Organically grown hemp accessories, bags, and apparel.

ALTERNATIVES TO LEATHER
& OTHER ANIMAL PRODUCTS

Eddie Bauer
800-625-7935
www.eddiebauer.com
Nonleather laptop briefcases, luggage, duffle bags, day packs, and briefcases.

Emerica
949-460-2020
www.emericaskate.com
Several styles of nonleather skateboarding shoes.

Enzo Angiolini
877-835-7732
Some fashionable professional nonleather women's shoes.

És Footwear
www.esfootwear.com
Several styles of nonleather skateboarding shoes.

Etnies
949-460-2020
www.etnies.com
Several styles of nonleather skateboarding shoes.

Etonic Shoes
800-225-6601
customer-relations@spalding.com
www.spalding.com
Synthetic athletic shoes.

EVOLVE
714-891-0555
evolv@evolveclimbing.com
www.evolvesports.com
Nonleather rock-climbing shoes.

Fabulous Furs
800-848-4650
custserv@fabulousfurs.com
www.fabulousfurs.com
Faux fur coats.

Fallen Footwear
760-599-2999
info@fallenfootwear.com
www.fallenfootwear.com
Several styles of nonleather skateboarding shoes.

Fantasia Wear
800-850-3268
sales@fantasiawear.com
www.fantasiawear.com
Sexy vinyl dresses, corsets, skirts, pants, catsuits, stilettos, boots, and thigh-high boots.

Fashion Bug
www.fashionbug.com
Nonleather shoes.

Fast Company
800-459-2239
info@dragginjeans.com
www.dragginjeans.com
Denim protective motercycle gear.

Faux Fur Fashions
info@fauxfurfashion.com
www.fauxfurfashion.com
Faux fur coats for men and women, clothing, shoes, furniture, throws, and accessories.

Fila
888-FILA-NET
filastore@fila-usa.com
www.fila.com
Synthetic athletic shoes.

Five Ten
909-798-4222
custserv@fiveten.com
www.fiveten.com
Nonleather rock-climbing shoes include the "Dragon," "Anasazi Velcro," and "Anasazi Lace-Up."

Fogdog Sports
800-624-2017
www.fogdog.com
Synthetic athletic shoes, golf gloves, footballs, basketballs, and softballs.

FredaLA.com
888-987-5678
customerservice@fredala.com
fredala.com
Nonleather bags.

Frederick's of Hollywood
800-323-9525
custserv@fredericks.com
www.fredericks.com
Clothing with faux fur, pleather pants and skirts, faux suede skirts, and nonleather shoes and boots.

Funk e Feet
518-489-4387
funkefeet@funkefeet.com
www.funkefeet.com
Nonleather shoes marked with a cow symbol for easy identification.

Garmont, USA, Inc.
802-658-8322
info@garmontusa.com
www.garmontusa.com
Nonleather hiking boots.

Giali USA
919-877-8108
gialiuk@compuserve.com
www.motorcycle-uk.com/gialiuk.html
Nonleather motorcycle jackets and shirts.

Globe
888-4-GLOBES
usa@globeshoes.com
www.globeshoes.com
Several styles of nonleather skateboarding shoes.

G.O. Max
800-590-8888
gomaxjy@flash.net
www.gomax.com
Trendy nonleather women's shoes.

Gravis Footwear
800-223-7450
info@gravisfootwear.com
www.gravisfootwear.com
Nonleather bags and athletic shoes.

Green Shoes
011 44 18 0386 4997
info@greenshoes.co.uk
www.greenshoes.co.uk
Men's, women's, and children's shoes, boots, and casual sandals custom-made from nonleather materials.

Grishko
www.grishko.com
Nonleather technique ballet shoes.

Harley-Davidson
800-LUV2RIDE or 414-343-4056 for international catalog requests
www.harleydavidson.com
Nonleather motorcycle coats, gloves, saddle bags, and fork bags.

HatShack.com
888-HATSHACK
alex@hatshack.com
www.hatshack.com
Nonleather cowboy hats.

Hawk Footwear
www.hawkshoes.com
Several styles of nonleather skateboarding shoes.

Heavenly Soles
612-822-2169
info@heavenlysoles.com
www.heavenlysoles.com
Shoes from Vegetarian Shoes.

The Hempery
800-BUY-HEMP
sales@hempery.com
www.hempery.com
Hemp sandals, bags, purses, belts, wallets, and bike bags.

Hot Topic
626-839-4681
www.hottopic.com
Nonleather bags, belts, accessories, clothing, boots, shoes, and sneakers.

IPath
info@ipathtrade.com
www.ipath.com
Several styles of nonleather skateboarding shoes.

Jack Spade
212-625-1820
www.jackspade.com
Designer nonleather bags in shoulder/bicycle- and courier/briefcase-styles.

JCPenney
800-322-1189
www.jcpenney.com
Nonleather bags and shoes.

Jeanne Lottie
416-968-2299
www.jeannelottie.com
PVC bags, cosmetics cases, cell phone cases, coin purses, and wallets.

Joe Rocket Sports Gear
800-635-6103
joerocket@joerocket.com
www.joerocket.com
Nonleather motorcycle jackets, gloves, and pants.

Karen Lukacs
520-250-4260
kjlukacs@worldnet.att.net
www.karenlukacsonline.com
Nonleather purses.

Kate Spade
800-519-3778
www.katespade.com
Nonleather designer handbags, totes, and shoes.

Keds
800-680-0966
keds@natcat.com
www.keds.com
Synthetic athletic shoes.

Kmart
866-KMART4U
kmartccn@kmart.com
www.bluelight.com
Wide variety of synthetic leather shoes.

Kohl's
866-887-8884
www.kohls.com
Nonleather bags, shoes, and winter boots and faux shearling jackets.

LaCrosse Boots
800-323-BOOT
www.lacrosse-outdoors.com
Several styles of rubber boots: insulated, non-insulated, and steel-toed.

The Last Resort
561-586-3700
info@thelastresort.net
www.thelastresort.nu
Nonleather shoes, bags, and Creepers.

L.E.I. Jeans
212-242-9356
info@leiapparel.com
www.lifeenergyintelligence.com
Trendy nonleather shoes.

Life Stride
888-233-6743
www.lifestride.com
Synthetic pumps, boots, and sandals.

ALTERNATIVES TO LEATHER
& OTHER ANIMAL PRODUCTS

Lip Service
866-DO-LIPPY
webkatt@lip-service.com
www.lip-service.com
Pleather pants, tops, dresses, jackets, coats,
vests, and hats.

Liz Claiborne
212-354-4900
www.lizclaiborne.com
Synthetic shoes in several styles.

L.L. Bean
800-441-5713
www.llbean.com
Nonleather ice and hockey skates, bags,
athletic shoes, boots, and coats.

Macbeth Shoes
760-431-5577
info@macbethshoes.com
www.macbethshoecompany.com
"The Eliot" synthetic shoe.

Madeline Stuart Shoes
800-368-7463
info@madelineshoes.com
www.madelineshoes.com
Fashionable women's shoes made from linen,
microfiber, and other synthetic materials.

Mad Rock
503-797-1952
info@madrockclimbing.com
www.madrockclimbing.com
Nonleather rock-climbing shoes.

Marsee Products
800-293-2400
marsee@marseeproducts.com
www.marseeproducts.com
Nonleather motorcycle jackets, pants, and
cooling vests.

Masseys
800-280-0846
sales@masseys.com
www.emasseys.com
Nonleather flats, pumps, and other shoes.

Morrco Pet Supply
800-575-1451
www.morrco.com
Fancy nonleather dog collars.

MotoLiberty
800-214-RACE
sales@motoliberty.com
www.motoliberty.com
Nonleather motorcycle jackets.

Motonation
877-789-4940
sales@motonation.com
www.motonation.com
Variety of nonleather motorcycle boots.

Motoport/Cycleport
800-777-6499
motoport@motoport.com
www.motoport.com
Nonleather motorcycle pants, jackets,
accessories, and road racing suits.

Mudd Jeans
www.muddjeans.com
Nonleather bags, belts, and shoes.

Nailers, Inc.
619-562-2215
Nonleather tool belts, nail bags, and kneepads
made from Dupont's Cordura® fabric.

Naturalizer
866-SHOES4U
naturalizer@brownshoe.com
www.naturalizeronline.com
Nonleather wedge pumps and snow boots.

New Balance
800-343-1395
www.newbalance.com
Several synthetic styles of athletic shoes.

NewGrip.com
800-834-2695
newgrip@juno.com
www.newgrip.com
Nonleather weight-lifting gloves.

Nike
800-344-6453
www.nikebiz.com
Men's and women's shoes made with synthetic uppers, including soccer and golf cleats, and children's and babies' shoes.

99X
212-460-8599
NY99X@hotmail.com
www.99Xny.com
Nonleather sneakers, shoes, wallets, and belts.

Nine West
800-999-1877
www.ninewest.com
Nonleather shoes, belts, wallets, purses, bags, and other accessories.

Northwave
206-762-2955
nwtim@northwave.it
www.northwave.com
Synthetic cycling shoes include "Stealth," "Supercompact," and "Team MTB."

Off Broadway Shoes
678-393-008
www.offbroadwayshoes.com
Nonleather shoes and bags.

Olympia Sports
800-645-6124
info@olympiagloves.com
www.olympiagloves.com
Nonleather riding gloves.

1154 LILL
773-292-6310
lillweb@1154lill.com
www.1154lill.com
Stylish nonleather bags.

The OOOF Ball Company
800-356-6631
ooof@ooofball.com
www.ooofball.com
Nonleather medicine balls that bounce and float.

Osiris
858-874-4970
info@osirisshoes.com
www.osirisshoes.com
Many styles of nonleather skateboarding shoes.

Pamela McCoy
800-884-2212
www.shopnbc.com
Faux fur coats and hats, available through ShopNBC.

Paul Frank
949-515-7950
pfr@paulfrank.com
www.paulfrank.com
Vinyl wallets, bags, coin purses, belts, and backpacks.

Payless Shoe Source
877-474-6379
www.payless.com
Widest selection of synthetic leather shoes and bags available.

Perfect Image
615-260-4520
Faux fur accessories.

Prima Royale Shoes
626-960-8388
primashoes@aol.com
Nonleather shoes for women.

PUMA
888-565-PUMA
customeremail@puma.com
www.puma.com
Some synthetic athletic shoes, including baseball and soccer cleats.

Purrfect Fur
619-291-4419
laball@purrfect-fur.com
www.purrfect-fur.com
Faux fur clip-on collars, cuffs, and accessories.

Rack Room Shoes
www.rackroomshoes.com
Nonleather shoes and bags.

ALTERNATIVES TO LEATHER
& OTHER ANIMAL PRODUCTS

Reebok
800-843-4444
www.reebok.com
Several synthetic athletic shoes, including football, baseball, and soccer cleats.

REI
800-426-4840
www.rei.com
Adidas "Adventure" sandals, Teva sports sandals, Merrell sports sandals, Nike sports sandals, nonleather belts, biking gloves, boots, and watchbands.

Resophonic Outfitters
301-733-8271
sales@beardguitars.com
www.beardguitars.com
Nonleather guitar straps.

Road Gear
719-547-4572
postmaster@roadgear.com
www.roadgear.com
Nonleather motorcycle pants.

Road Runner Sports
800-636-3560
www.roadrunnersports.com
Nonleather running shoes include Brooks, Asics, New Balance, Saucony, Reebok, Mizuno, Adidas, and Etonic.

Roaman's
800-274-7130
Several leather-like and canvas casual and dress shoes.

Rocket Dog
213-629-9266
info@rocketdog.co.uk
www.rocketdog.co.uk
Trendy nonleather shoes.

Sam & Libby
770-801-1200
samandlibby@maxwellshoe.com
www.samandlibby.com
Nonleather shoes for women.

Santana Canada Footwear
888-SANTANA
Waterproof nonleather boots and shoes in a variety of styles.

Saucony, Inc.
800-365-4933
feedback@saucony.com
www.saucony.com
Several synthetic athletic shoes.

SiDi USA
800-991-0070
info@sidiusa.com
www.sidiusa.com
Synthetic cycling shoes.

Skechers
800-746-3411
info@skechers.com
www.skechers.com
Lots of boots, as well as canvas and rubber shoes.

Snaz75.com
customerservice@snaz75.com
www. snaz75.com
Sexy nonleather boots, shoes, and sandals.

Spalding Sports
800-SPALDING
customer-relations@spalding.com
www.spalding.com
Synthetic volleyballs, basketballs, softballs, soccer balls, and footballs.

Steve Madden
888-SMADDEN
customerassistance@smadden.com
www.stevemadden.com
Many nonleather women's shoes.

Sunsports
800-308-HEMP
Hemp clothing, hats, shoes, and packs.

Sweet Herb
718-667-0363
kathleen@sweetherb.com
www.sweetherb.com
Faux fur capes, boas, stoles, vests, hats, and
bridal accessories.

Target
888-304-4000
www.target.com
Wide variety of synthetic shoes, bags, wallets,
and more.

Teknic
616-866-3722 (East Coast)
949-363-0836 (West Coast)
tekniccustserv@ssltd.org
www.teknicgear.com
Textile jackets, pants, gloves, and boots for
motorcycling.

Teva
800-367-8382
customerservice@tevasandals.com
www.teva.com
Nonleather sports shoes, sandals, and
clothing.

Thorowgood, Ltd.
011 44 19 2271 1676
sales@thorowgood.co.uk
www.thorowgood.com
Synthetic saddles.

Timberland
800-445-5545
info@timberland.com
www.timberland.com
Clothing, outerwear, backpacks, and bags.

Tomorrow's World
800-229-7571
cs@tomorrowsworld.com
www.tomorrowsworld.com
Nonleather clothing, shoes, belts, bags, and
organic hemp products.

Tour Master
www.tourmaster.com
Nonleather motorcycle jackets, pants, one-
piece suits, gloves, and bags.

Tretorn
tretornus@tretorn.com
www.tretorn.com
Canvas tennis-style shoes.

Unlisted by Kenneth Cole
800-KENCOLE
www.kencole.com
Line of leather-like shoes, belts, and handbags
for women.

Vans
800-826-7800
custserv@vansshoes.com
www.vans.com
Canvas, linen, and flannel Oxfords, mules,
Mary Janes, and nonleather skateboarding
shoes.

Vereschagin Designs
www.sonya-v.com
Faux fur; day, evening, and outer wear;
sweaters; and faux leather bags.

V Sports
800-765-4200
Synthetic soccer balls.

Weatherproof Garment Company
212-695-7716
info@weatherproofgarment.com
www.weatherproofgarment.com
Weatherproof nonleather outerwear for
men, women, and children.

Wellington House
800-624-8258
Wide variety of conservative nonleather shoe
styles.

Wild Pair
314-621-0699
Stylish nonleather shoes and boots.

Willie & Max
847-356-7763
info@willieandmax.com
www.willieandmax.com
Nonleather saddle bags.

ALTERNATIVES TO LEATHER
& OTHER ANIMAL PRODUCTS

Wilson Sporting Goods Company
773-714-6400
info@team.wilsonsports.com
www.wilsonsports.com
Nonleather footballs, etc.

Wintec
www.wintec.net.au
Synthetic saddles.

XOXO
866-201-1295
www.xoxo.com
Nonleather bags and wallets.

Yak Pak
800-2-YAKPAK
customerservice@yakpak.com
www.yakpak.com
Synthetic bags.

Yamaha Motor Corporation
800-88-Yamaha
www.yamaha-motor.com
Nonleather riding gloves.

Zappos.com
cs@zappos.com
www.zappos.com
Wide variety of nonleather shoes.

fashion victim
leather is dead skin—think about it ...

CowsAreCool.com PeTA

Athletic Shoes

Active Soles
Adidas
Asics
Avia
Converse
Etonic Shoes
Fila
Fogdog Sports⊟
Gravis Footwear
Keds
L.L. Bean
New Balance
Nike
Payless Shoe
    Source
Puma
Reebok
Road Runner
    Sports⊟
Saucony, Inc.
Skechers
Teva
Tretorn
Vans

Bags

All Vegan
Alternative
    Outfitters
Bagg Lady
    Handbags
Bulge
Cedar Key
    Canvas
Charlotte Russe
Chrome Bags
Crystalyn Kae
Diesel
Dragonfly
DSW
Ecolution
Eddie Bauer
Faux
Freerangers
FredaLa.com
Gloria Gerber
GoodGoth.com
Gravis Footwear
Helen Powers
The Hempery

Hot Topic
Jack Spade
JCPenney
Jeanne Lottie
Karen Lukacs
Kate Spade
Kohl's
The Last Resort
Little Packrats
L.L. Bean
M. Avery Designs
Mudd Jeans
N/A Designs
Nedra Made It
Nine West
Off Broadway Shoes
1154 LILL
OTSU
Pangea⊟
Paul Frank
Payless Shoe
    Source
Queen Bee
    Creations
Rack Room Shoes
R.E. Load Baggage, Inc.
Slim Pawn Handmade
    Handbags
Sparkle Craft
Splaff Flops
Stella McCartney
Target
Timberland
Timbuk2 Designs
Tom Bihn⊟
Tomorrow's World
Truth
Unlisted by
    Kenneth Cole
Used Rubber USA
Vegan Essentials
Vegan Wares⊟
TheVegetarian
    Site.com
Vereschagin
    Designs
Via Vegan⊟
Vulcana Bags
XOXO
Yak Pak⊟

Balls

Fogdog Sports⊟
Ooof Ball
    Company
Spalding Sports
V Sports
Wilson Sporting
    Goods
    Company

Baseball Gloves

Heartland Products, Ltd.

Belts

All Vegan
Alternative
    Outfitters
Crystalyn Kae
Ethical Wares⊟
Freerangers
Heartland
    Products, Ltd.
The Hempery
Hot Topic
INOPIA Footwear
MooShoes⊟
Mudd Jeans
99x
Nine West
NoBull Footwear
OTSU
Pangea⊟
Paul Frank
REI
Shoes with Souls
Sparkle Craft
Splaff Flops
Tomorrow's World
Truth
Unlisted by
    Kenneth Cole
Vegan Essentials
Veganline
Vegan Wares⊟
Vegetarian Shoes

Biking Gloves

REI

QUICK REFERENCE GUIDE

Bowling Shoes
Dexter Shoes

Cleats
Adidas
Dexter Shoes
Nike
Puma
Reebok

**Companion Animal
Accessories**
Morrco Pet Supply
Nedra Made It
Vegan Wares

Cycling Shoes
Northwave
SiDi USA

Dance Shoes
Capezio
Cynthia King Dance
Grishko
Vegan Wares ✇

Dress/Casual Shoes
Aerosoles
Alloy
All Vegan
Alternative
    Outfitters
Anywhere Shoes
Á Propos ...
    Conversations
Bakers Shoe
    Store
Beyond Skin
Birkenstock
    Footwear
Burlington Coat Factory
Charlotte Russe
Chinese Laundry
    Shoes
Cloudwalkers
Coldwater Creek
Crocs
Delia's ✇
Diesel
Dragonfly
DSW

Earth
Enzo Angiolini
Ethical Wares ✇
Fantasia Wear
Fashion Bug
Frederick's of
    Hollywood
Freerangers
Funk e Feet
G.O. Max
GoodGoth.com
Green Shoes
Heartland
    Products, Ltd. ✇
Heavenly Soles
The Hempery
Hot Topic
JCPenney
Kate Spade
Kmart
Kohl's
The Last Resort
L.E.I. Jeans
Life Stride
Liz Claiborne
Madeline Stuart
    Shoes
Masseys
MooShoes ✇
Mudd Jeans
Naturalizer
99x
Nine West
NoBull Footwear
Off Broadway Shoes
OTSU
Pangea ✇
Payless Shoe
    Source
Prima Royale
    Shoes
Rack Room Shoes
REI
Roaman's
Rocket Dog
Sam & Libby
Santana Canada
Shoes with Souls
Skechers
Snaz75.com
Splaff Flops
Stella McCartney
Steve Madden

Sunsports
Target
Teva
Tomorrow's World
Unlisted by
    Kenneth Cole
Vans
Vegan Essentials
Veganline
Vegan Wares ✇
Vegetarian Shoes
TheVegetarian
    Site.com
Wellington House
Wild Pair
Zappos.com

Faux Fur
Bootzwalla
Burlington Coat Factory
Charlotte Russe
Charly Calder
    International ✇
Comfurts by
    Ken Alan
Coquette Faux Furriers ✇
Dillard's
Fabulous Furs ✇
Faux
Faux Fur Fashions
Frederick's of
    Hollywood
Fur Replicas
Pamela McCoy
Perfect Image
Posh Pelts
Premium Furs
Purrfect Fur
Sweet Herb
Vereschagin
    Designs

Guitar Straps
Di Marzio, Inc.
Këpur
Pangea
Resophonic
    Outfitters
Sparkle Craft
Vegan Wares

Hiking/Work Boots
Bata Shoe
   Company, Inc.
Ethical Wares ☞
Five Ten
Garmont, USA, Inc.
Heartland
   Products, Ltd. ☞
LaCrosse Boots
Last Resort ☞
NoBull Footwear
Pangea ☞
REI
Santana Canada
   Footwear
Vegetarian Shoes

Ice and Hockey Skates
L.L. Bean

Motorcycle Apparel
Aerostich/Rider
   Warehouse
Alpine Stars
Competition
   Accessories
Dennis Kirk
Fast Company
Giali USA
Harley-Davidson
Heartland
   Products, Ltd.
Joe Rocket
   Sports Gear
Marsee Products
MotoLiberty
Motonation
Motoport/Cycleport
Olympia Sports
Road Gear
Teknic
Tour Master
Vegetarian Shoes
Willie & Max
Yamaha Motor
   Corporation

Rock-Climbing Shoes
EVOLVE
Five Ten

Saddles
Thorowgood, Ltd.
Wintec

Skateboarding Shoes
Circa
Emerica
És Footwear
Etnies
Globe
Hawk Footwear
INOPIA Footwear
IPath
Macbeth Shoes
Osiris
Savier
Vans

Snowboarding Boots
Airwalk
Burton
   Snowboards

Snow Boots
Kohl's
Naturalizer
Payless Shoe
   Source

Tool Belts
Nailers, Inc.

Wallets
Alternative
   Outfitters
Ductbill
The Hempery
INOPIA Footwear
Jeanne Lottie
MooShoes ☞
99x
Nine West
NoBull Footwear
OTSU
Pangea ☞
Paul Frank
Queen Bee
   Creations
Target
Used Rubber USA
Vegan Essentials

Vegan Wares ☞
TheVegetarian
   Site.com
Vulcana Bags
Wal-Mart Stores, Inc.
XOXO

Weight-Lifting Gloves
NewGrip.com

Western-Style Boots
Heartland
   Products, Ltd. ☞

HEALTH CHARITIES:
HELPING OR HURTING?

When you donate to a charity, do you know where the money actually goes? Could your gift be contributing to animal suffering?

Some health charities ask for donations to help people with diseases and disabilities yet spend the money to bankroll horrific experiments on dogs, rabbits, rats, mice, primates, hamsters, pigs, ferrets, frogs, fish, guinea pigs, sheep, birds, and other animals. While human health needs cry out for attention and so many people are going without medical care, animal experimentation enriches laboratories and scientists but drains money from relevant and effective projects that could really help save lives.

Healing Without Hurting

Instead of ravaging animals' bodies for cures for human diseases, compassionate charities focus their research where the best hope of treatment lies: with humans.

Human volunteers, clinical studies, autopsy reports, and statistical and epidemiological analyses provide useful data on people with diseases and disabilities. Human cell cultures and tissue studies, *in vitro* tests, and artificial human "skin" and "eyes" mimic the body's natural properties and provide scientists with less expensive alternatives to animal tests. In addition, a number of sophisticated computer virtual organs serve as accurate models of human body parts.

Compassionate, modern charities know that we can improve treatments through up-to-date, non-animal methods, and they fund only non-animal research, leading to real progress in the prevention and treatment of disease.

Tal Ronnen/PETA

HEALTH CHARITIES THAT **DON'T FUND** ANIMAL EXPERIMENTS ▐███████████████

What Types of Charities Are on the 'Don't Test' List?

Health charities and service organizations that do not conduct or fund experiments on animals are included on the "don't test" list. These organizations deal with human health issues ranging from birth defects to cancer to substance abuse. Some fund non-animal research to find treatments and cures for diseases and disabilities, while others provide services and direct care to people living with physical or mental ailments.

How Does a Charity Get on the List?

The charities on this list have provided written assurance or have signed a statement of assurance put forth by the Council on Humane Giving certifying that neither they nor their affiliated organizations conduct or fund any experiments on animals and that they will not do so in the future. The Council on Humane Giving encompasses nine animal protection organizations, including PETA and the Physicians Committee for Responsible Medicine. The Council was formed to help humane health charities publicize their cruelty-free policies and to allow donors to easily identify such charities with the Humane Charity Seal of Approval. Charities marked with a check (✓) are currently observing a moratorium on (i.e., current suspension of) animal experiments.

Please contact the Council on Humane Giving at 202-686-2210, extension 335, or visit www.humaneseal.org for more information.

Contact PETA if you know the address of a charity that is not listed, including local health service organizations. PETA will be happy to inquire about a charity's animal-testing policy, but we also encourage you to inquire yourself, as it is important for charities to hear directly from compassionate citizens who are opposed to animal testing.

The following health charities and service organizations do not conduct or fund animal experiments. They may deal with several issues, including nonhealth-related issues, but they are listed according to their primary health focus. For more information on the programs and activities of an organization, please contact that organization directly.

HEALTH CHARITIES THAT **DON'T FUND** ANIMAL EXPERIMENTS

AIDS/HIV

AIDS Coalition of Cape Breton
106 Townsend St., Ste.10
Sydney, NS B1P 6H1
Canada
902-567-1766
www.accb.ns.ca

The Angel Connection, Inc.
3 Executive Dr.
P.O. Box 9123
Greystone Park, NJ 07950
973-898-0048
www.theangelconnection.org

Caring for Babies with AIDS
5922 Comey Ave.
Los Angeles, CA 90034
323-931-1440

Charlotte HIV/AIDS Network, Inc. (CHAN)
3880 Tamiami Trl., #E
Port Charlotte, FL 33952
941-625-6650
941-625-AIDS

Chicago House
1925 N. Clayburn, Ste. 401
Chicago, IL 60614
773-248-5200

Children's Immune Disorder
16888 Greenfield Rd.
Detroit, MI 48235-3707
313-837-7800

Concerned Citizens for Humanity
3580 Main St., Ste. 115
Hartford, CT 06120-1121
860-560-0833

Design Industries Foundation Fighting AIDS (DIFFA)
147 W. 24th St., 7th Fl.
New York, NY 10011
212-727-3100
www.diffa.org

Gay Men's Health Crisis
119 W. 24th St.
New York, NY 10011
212-367-1000
www.gmhc.org

Health Cares Exchange Initiative, Inc.
7100 N. Ashland Ave.
Chicago, IL 60626
773-509-6402
www.hcei.org

HIV Network of Edmonton Society
10550-102 Street
Edmonton, AB T5H 2T3
Canada
780-488-5742
www.hivedmonton.com

Joshua Tree Feeding Program, Inc.
1601 W. Indian School Rd.
Phoenix, AZ 85015-5233
602-264-0223

Loving Arms
P.O. Box 3368
Memphis, TN 38173
901-725-6730

Miracle House of New York
80 Eighth Ave., Ste. 709
New York, NY 10011
212-989-7790
www.miraclehouse.org

Phoenix Shanti Group, Inc.
2020 W. Indian School Rd. #50
Phoenix, AZ 85015
602-279-0008

Puerto Rico Community Network for Clinical Research on AIDS
P.O. Box 20850
San Juan, PR 00928-0850
787-753-9443

ARTHRITIS

Arthritis Research Institute of America
300 S. Duncan Ave., Ste. 240
Clearwater, FL 33755
727-461-4054
www.preventarthritis.org

The Arthritis Trust of America, a.k.a. The Rheumatoid Disease Foundation
7376 Walker Rd.
Fairview, TN 37062-8141
615-799-1002
www.arthritistrust.org

BIRTH DEFECTS

Birth Defect Research for Children, Inc.
930 Woodcock Rd.
Ste. 225
Orlando, FL 32803
800-313-2232
www.birthdefects.org

Easter Seals
230 W. Monroe St.
Ste. 1800
Chicago, IL 60606
800-221-6827
www.easter-seals.org

Easter Seal Society
1185 Eglington Ave. E.
Ste. 706
Toronto, ON M4P 2Y3
Canada
416-932-8382
www.easterseals.ca

Little People's Research Fund, Inc.
80 Sister Pierre Dr.
Towson, MD 21204
800-232-5773
www.lprf.org

National Craniofacial Association
P.O. Box 11082
Chattanooga, TN 37401
800-332-2373
www.faces-cranio.org

Puerto Rico Down Syndrome Foundation
P.O. Box 195273
San Juan, PR 00919-5273
www.sindromedown.org

Spina Bifida Association of America
4590 MacArthur Blvd. N.W.
Ste. 250
Washington, DC 20007-4226
800-621-3141
www.sbaa.org

Warner House
1023 E. Chapman Ave.
Fullerton, CA 92831
714-441-2600
www.warnerhouse.com

BLIND/VISUALLY IMPAIRED

American Action Fund for Blind Children and Adults
1800 Johnson St.
Baltimore, MD 21230
410-659-9315
www.actionfund.org

American Association of the Deaf-Blind
814 Thayer Ave., Ste. 302
Silver Spring, MD 20910-4500

Collier County Association for the Blind
4701 Golden Gate Pkwy.
Naples, FL 34116
239-649-1122
www.naples.net/social/ccab

Connecticut Institute for the Blind/Oak Hill
120 Holcomb St.
Hartford, CT 06112-1589
860-242-2274
www.ciboakhill.org

Deaf-Blind Service Center
1620 18th Ave., Ste. 200
Seattle, WA 98122
206-323-9178
www.seattledbsc.org

Foundation for the Junior Blind
5200 Angeles Vista Blvd.
Los Angeles, CA 90043
323-295-4555
www.fjb.org

Helen Keller Worldwide
352 Park Ave. S., Ste. 1200
New York, NY 10010
877-535-5374
www.hkworld.org

International Eye Foundation
10801 Connecticut Ave.
Kensington, MD 20895
240-290-0263
www.iefusa.org

Living Skills Center for Visually Impaired
2430 Rd. 20, Apt. 112
San Pablo, CA 94806-5006
510-234-4984

National Association for the Visually Handicapped
22 W. 21st St.
New York, NY 10010
212-889-3141

National Federation of the Blind, Inc.
1800 Johnson St.
Baltimore, MD 21230
410-659-9314
www.nfb.org

Radio Information Service
2100 Wharton St., Ste. 140
Pittsburgh, PA 15203
412-488-3944
www.readingservice.org

Vision Resource Center
1414 Bragg Blvd.
Fayetteville, NC 28303
910-483-2719

VISIONS/Services for the Blind and Visually Impaired
500 Greenwich St., 3rd Fl.
New York, NY 10013-1354
212-625-1616
www.visionsvcb.org

Washington Volunteer Readers for the Blind
901 G St. N.W.
Washington, DC 20001
202-727-2142

HEALTH CHARITIES THAT **DON'T FUND** ANIMAL EXPERIMENTS

BLOOD

Canadian Red Cross
(Croix-Rouge canadienne)
170 Metcalfe St., Ste. 300
Ottawa, ON K2P 2P2
Canada
613-740-1900
www.redcross.ca

Michigan Community Blood Centers
P.O. Box 1704
Grand Rapids, MI 49501-1704
866-MIBLOOD
www.miblood.org

BURNS

Children's Burn Foundation
4929 Van Nuys Blvd.
Sherman Oaks, CA 91403
818-907-2822

CANCER

American Breast Cancer Foundation
1055 Taylor Ave., Ste. 201
Baltimore, MD 21286
410-825-9388
www.abcf.org

A.P. John Institute for Cancer Research
67 Arch St.
Greenwich, CT 06830
203-661-2571
www.apjohncancerinstitute.org

Avon Breast Cancer Crusade
Avon Products Foundation
1345 Ave. of the Americas
New York, NY 10105
212-282-5666
www.avoncrusade.com

The Breast Cancer Fund
1388 Sutter St., Ste. 400
San Francisco, CA 94109
415-346-8223
www.breastcancerfund.org

Calvary Fund, Inc.
Calvary Hospital
1740 Eastchester Rd.
Bronx, NY 10461
877-4-CALVARY
www.calvaryhospital.org

Cancer Care Services
605 W. Magnolia
Ft. Worth, TX 76104
817-921-0653

Cancer Fund of America, Inc.
2901 Breezewood Ln.
Knoxville, TN 37921-1099
800-441-1664
www.cfoa.org

The Cancer Project
c/o PCRM
5100 Wisconsin Ave. N.W. Ste. 400
Washington, DC 20016
202-686-2210
www.cancerproject.org

Cancer Treatment Research Foundation
3150 Salt Creek Ln., Ste. 122
Arlington Heights, IL 60005-1087
847-342-7443
www.ctrf.org

Children's Cancer Association
7524 S.W. Macadam, Ste. B
Portland, OR 97219
503-244-3141
www.childrenscancerassociation.org

Danville Cancer Association, Inc.
2323 Riverside Dr.
Danville, VA 24540-4271
434-792-3700

The Garland Appeal
37 Meteor Tr.
Andover, NJ 07821
973-347-8808
www.garlandappealusa.com
or
65 Marathon House
200 Marylebone Rd.
London NW1 5PL
England
011 44 17 2845 4820
www.garlandappeal.com

Gilda Radner Familial Ovarian Cancer Registry
Rosewell Park Cancer Institute
Elm and Carlton Sts.
Buffalo, NY 14263-0001
716-845-8059
800-682-7426
www.ovariancancer.com

Lymphoma Foundation of America
814 N. Garfield St.
Arlington, VA 22201
703-875-9800
www.lymphomahelp.org

Miracle House of New York
80 Eighth Ave., Ste. 709
New York, NY 10011
212-989-7790
www.miraclehouse.org

National Children's Cancer Society
1015 Locust, Ste. 1040
St. Louis, MO 63101
314-241-1600

Be a
**Bunny's
Honey**

Buy Cruelty-Free

Save a bunny's cute cotton tail by buying lip gloss, shower gel, toothpaste, and other products from companies that have banned animal tests **forever**.

More than 500 companies, such as Bonne Bell, Hello Kitty Cosmetics, mark, Revlon, and Urban Decay Cosmetics, conduct safety tests using everything from computers to simulated human skin—but no animals!

Visit peta2.com for free stickers, DVDs, and a list of cruelty-free companies. **peta2**.com

HEALTH CHARITIES THAT **DON'T FUND** ANIMAL EXPERIMENTS

Quest Cancer Research
Unite E3, Seebed Business
Center
Coldharbour Rd., Harlow
Essex CM19 5AF
England
011 44 12 7945 1359

Share
1501 Broadway, Ste. 1720
New York, NY 10036
212-719-0364

Skin Cancer Foundation
245 Fifth Ave., Ste. 1403
New York, NY 10016
800-754-6490
www.skincancer.org

Tomorrows Children's Fund
Hackensack University
Medical Center
30 Prospect Ave.
Hackensack, NJ 07601
201-996-5500
www.atcfkid.com

United Cancer Reserach Society
3545 20th St.
Highland, CA 92346-4542
800-222-1533
www.unitedcancer.org

CARDIOVASCULAR

American Pediatric Heart Fund
16024 Manchester Rd.
Ste. 200
St. Louis, MO 63011
636-594-2202
www.aphfund.org

Lown Cardiovascular Research Foundation
21 Longwood Ave.
Brookline, MA 02446
617-732-1318
www.lowncenter.org

Palm Springs Stroke Activity Center
2800 E. Alejo St.
Palm Springs, CA 92263-0355
760-323-7676

Save a Child's Heart Foundation
11400 Rockville Pike
Ste. 800
Rockville, MD 20852-3004
301-618-4593
www.saveachildsheart.com

Stroke Survivors Support Group of Pueblo
710½ E. Mesa Ave.
Pueblo, CO 81006
719-583-8498

CHILDREN

Birth Defect Research for Children, Inc.
930 Woodcock Rd.
Ste. 225
Orlando, FL 32803
800-313-2232
www.birthdefects.org

Carroll County Health and Home Care Services
Carroll County Complex
Ossipee, NH 03864
800-499-4171

Children's Burn Foundation
4929 Van Nuys Blvd.
Sherman Oaks, CA 91403
818-907-2822
800-949-8898
www.childburn.org

Children's Diagnostic Center, Inc.
2100 Pleasant Ave.
Hamilton, OH 45015
513-868-1562

Children's Health Environmental Coalition (CHEC)
P.O. Box 1540
Princeton, NJ 08542
609-252-1915
www.checnet.org

Children's Wish Foundation International
8615 Roswell Rd.
Atlanta, GA 30350-4867
800-323-WISH
www.childrenswish.org

Crestwood Children's Center
2075 Scottsville Rd.
Rochester, NY 14623-2098
716-436-4442
www.hillside.com

Eagle Valley Children's Home
2300 Eagle Valley Ranch Rd.
Carson City, NV 89703
702-882-1188

Five Acres/The Boys' and Girls' Aid Society of Los Angeles
760 W. Mountain View St.
Altadena, CA 91001
626-798-6793
www.5acres.org

The Healing Species
P.O. Box 1202
Orangeburg, SC 29116-1202
803-535-6543
www.healingspecies.org

Miracle Flights
2756 N. Green Valley Pkwy.
Ste. 115
Green Valley, NV 89014-2100
702-261-0494
www.miracleflights.org

National Children's Cancer Society
1015 Locust, Ste. 1040
St. Louis, MO 63101
314-241-1600
800-532-6459
www.children-cancer.com

Pathfinder International
9 Galen St., Ste. 217
Watertown, MA 02172-4501
617-924-7200
www.pathfind.org

Rainbow Society of Alberta
6604 82nd Ave.
Edmonton, AB T6B 0E7
Canada
403-469-3306
www.rainbowsociety.ab.ca

Tomorrows Children's Fund
Hackensack University Medical Center
30 Prospect Ave.
Hackensack, NJ 07601
201-996-5500
www.atcfkid.com

UNICEF
333 E. 38th St.
New York, NY 10016
212-326-7303
www.unicef.org

DEAF/HEARING IMPAIRED

Be an Angel Fund
T.H. Rogers School
5840 San Felipe
Houston, TX 77057
713-917-3568

Better Hearing Institute
515 King St., Ste. 420
Alexandria, VA 22314
703-684-3391
www.betterhearing.org

Chicago Hearing Society
2001 W. Clybourn Ave.
Chicago, IL 60614
773-248-9121
www.chicagohearingsociety.org

Deaf Action Center
3115 Crestview Dr.
Dallas, TX 75235
214-521-0407
www.deafactioncentertexas.org

Deaf-Blind Service Center
2366 Eastlake Ave. E.
Ste. 206
Seattle, WA 98102
206-323-9178

Deaf Independent Living Association, Inc.
P.O. Box 4038
Salisbury, MD 21803-4038
410-742-5052
www.dila.org

Deaf Service Center of St. John's County
207 San Marco Ave., #38
St. Augustine, FL 32084-2762

Institute for Rehabilitation, Research, and Recreation, Inc.
P.O. Box 1025
Pendleton, OR 97801
541-276-2752

League for the Hard of Hearing
71 W. 23rd St.
New York, NY 10010-4162
917-305-7800
www.lhh.org

Minnesota State Academy for the Deaf
P.O. Box 308
Faribault, MN 55021
507-332-5402
www.msad.state.mn.us

DISABLED, DEVELOPMENTALLY

Achievements, Inc.
101 Mineral Ave.
Libby, MT 59923
406-293-8848

Adult Activity Services
307 E. Atlantic St.
Emporia, VA 23847
434-634-2124

Adult Training and Habilitation Center
311 Fairlawn Ave. W.
P.O. Box 600
Winsted, MN 55395
320-485-4191
www.athc.org

American Association on Mental Retardation
444 N. Capitol St. N.W.
Ste. 846
Washington, DC 20001-1512
800-424-3688
www.aamr.org

Association for Community Living
1 Carando Dr.
Springfield, MA 01104-3211
413-732-0531

Burnt Mountain Center
P.O. Box 337
Jasper, GA 30143
706-692-6016

Butler Valley, Inc.
380 12th St.
Arcata, CA 95521
707-822-0301

HEALTH CHARITIES THAT **DON'T FUND** ANIMAL EXPERIMENTS

Career Development Center
2110 W. Delaware
Fairfield, IL 62837
618-842-2691

Carroll Haven Achieving New Growth Experiences (CHANGE)
115 Stoner Ave.
Westminster, MD 21157-5443
410-876-2179

Christian Horizons
384 Arthur St. S.
Elmira, ON N3B 2P4
Canada
519-669-1571

Community Services
452 Delaware Ave.
Buffalo, NY 14202-1515
716-883-8888

Concerned Citizens for the Developmentally Disabled/Community Options
801-B Washington St.
P.O. Box 725
Chillicothe, MO 64601
660-646-0109

DeWitt County Human Resource Center
1150 Rte. 54 W.
Clinton, IL 61727
217-935-9496

Eagle Valley Children's Home
2300 Eagle Valley Ranch Rd.
Carson City, NV 89703
775-882-1188

EYAS Corporation
411 Scarlet Sage St.
Punta Gorda, FL 33950
941-575-2255

Hartville Meadows
P.O. Box 1055
Hartville, OH 44632
330-877-3694

Hebron Community, Inc.
P.O. Box 11
Lawrenceville, VA 23868

Hope House Foundation
801 Boush St., Ste. 302
Norfolk, VA 23510
757-625-6161
www.hope-house.org

Horizons Specialized Services, Inc.
405 Oak St.
Steamboat Springs, CO 80477-4867
973-879-4466

Kensington Community Corporation for Individual Dignity
5425 Oxford Ave.
Philadelphia, PA 19124
215-288-9797

Mountain Valley Developmental Services
P.O. Box 338
700 Mt. Sopris Dr.
Glenwood Springs, CO 81602
970-945-2306
www.mtnvalley.org

Mt. Angel Training Center and Residential Services
350 E. Church St.
Mt. Angel, OR 97362
503-845-9214

New Opportunities
1400 Seventh St.
Madison, IL 62060
618-876-3178

Nia Comprehensive Center for Developmental Disabilities
1808 S. State St.
Chicago, IL 60616
312-949-1808
800-NIA-1976

Opportunities Unlimited
3340 Marysville Blvd.
Sacramento, CA 95838
716-297-6400

Orange County Association for the Help of Retarded Citizens
249 Broadway
Newburgh, NY 12550
914-561-0670

Outlook Nashville, Inc.
3004 Tuggle Ave.
Nashville, TN 37211
615-834-7570

Phoenix Services, Inc.
221 W. Penn Ave.
Cleona, PA 17042
717-228-0400

Pleasant View Homes, Inc.
P.O. Box 426
Broadway, VA 22815
540-896-8255

Primrose Center
2733 S. Fern Creek Ave.
Orlando, FL 32806-5591
407-898-7201

RocVale Children's Home
4450 N. Rockton Ave.
Rockford, IL 61103
815-654-3050

San Antonio State School
P.O. Box 14700
San Antonio, TX 78214-0700
210-532-9610

Society to Aid Retarded, Inc. (S.T.A.R.)
P.O. Box 1075
Torrance, CA 90505

Southwest Human Development
202 E. Earll Dr., Ste. 140
Phoenix, AZ 85012
602-266-5976

St. Joseph Home, Inc.
1226 S. Sunbury Rd.
Westerville, OH 43081-9105

Swift County Developmental Achievement Center
2135 Minnesota Ave.
Bldg. 1
Benson, MN 56215
320-843-4201

DISABLED, PHYSICALLY

Access to Independence, Inc.
2345 Atwood Ave.
Madison, WI 53704-5602
608-242-8484

A+ Home Care, Inc.
8932 Old Cedar Ave. S.
Bloomington, MN 55425
800-603-7760

Association for Persons With Physical Disabilities of Windsor and Essex Counties
2001 Spring Garden Rd.
Windsor, ON N9E 3P8
Canada
519-969-8188

Friends
27 Forest St.
Parry Sound, ON P2A 2R2
Canada
705-746-5102

Getabout
P.O. Box 224
New Canaan, CT 06840-0224
203-972-7433

Hamilton District Society for Disabled Children
P.O. Box 2000, Station A
Sanitorium Rd.
Hamilton, ON L8N 3Z5
Canada
905-385-5391

Handicapped Housing Society of Alberta
205-3132 Parsons Rd.
Edmonton, AB T6N 1L6
Canada
780-451-1114

Independence Crossroads
8932 Old Cedar Ave. S.
Bloomington, MN 55425
952-854-8004

Michigan Wheelchair Athletic Association
14410 Vale Ct.
Sterling Heights, MI 48312
810-977-6123

Mower Council for the Handicapped
111 N. Main St.
Austin, MN 55912-3404
507-433-9609

North Bay and Area Centre for the Disabled
P.O. Box 137
409 Main St. E.
North Bay, ON P1B 8G8
Canada
705-474-3851

N.W.T. Council for Disabled Persons
P.O. Box 1387
Yellowknife, NT X1A 2P1
Canada
867-873-8230

Southwestern Independent Living Center
843 N. Main St.
Jamestown, NY 14701
716-661-3010

Special People, Inc.
Human Resources
City Hall
1420 Miner St.
Des Plaines, IL 60016

Tobias House Attendant Care, Inc.
695 Coxwell Ave., Ste. 611
Toronto, ON M4C 5R6
Canada
416-690-3185
www.tobiashouse.ca

United Amputee Services
557 Lagoon Dr.
Oviedo, FL 32765
407-359-5500

DISABLED, PHYSICALLY AND/OR DEVELOPMENTALLY

Be an Angel Fund
T.H. Rogers School
5840 San Felipe
Houston, TX 77057
713-917-3568

HEALTH CHARITIES THAT **DON'T FUND** ANIMAL EXPERIMENTS

Cheyenne Village Inc.
6275 Lehman Dr.
Colorado Springs, CO
80918-1433
719-592-0200

Comprehensive Advocacy, Inc.
4477 Emerald, Ste. B-100
Boise, ID 83706-2044
800-632-5125

Disability Rights Education & Defense Fund (DREDF)
2212 Sixth St.
Berkeley, CA 94710
510-644-2555

Disabled Resource Services
424 Pine St., Ste. 101
Fort Collins, CO 80524-2421
970-482-2700

Families Helping Families at the Crossroads of Louisiana
818 Main St., Ste. A
Pineville, LA 71360
318-445-7900
800-259-7200

Heartland Opportunity Center
Madera Center
323 N. E St.
Madera, CA 93638-3245
559-674-8828

Hodan Center, Inc.
941 W. Fountain St.
P.O. Box 212
Mineral Point, WI 53565
608-987-3336

Humboldt Community Access and Resource Center (HCAR)
P.O. Box 2010
Eureka, CA 95502

Indiana Rehabilitation Association
P.O. Box 44174
Indianapolis, IN 46244-0174
317-290-4320

Kinsmen Telemiracle Foundation
2217C Hanselman Ct., #C
Saskatoon, SK S7L 6A8
Canada
877-777-8979

Lifegains, Inc.
1601 S. Sterling St.
P.O. Drawer 1569
Morganton, NC 28680-1569
704-255-8845

Maidstone Foundation, Inc.
1225 Broadway
New York, NY 10001
828-433-7498

North Country Center for Independence
102 Sharron Ave.
Plattsburgh, NY 12901
518-563-9058
www.slic.com/ncci

Options Center for Independent Living
22 Heritage Plz., Ste. 107
Boubonnais, IL 60914-2503
815-936-0100

Ozarks Valley Community Service, Inc. (OVCS)
135 S. Main
Ironton, MO 63650-0156
573-546-2418

Rehabilitation Center
1439 Buffalo St.
Olean, NY 14760
716-372-8909

Rehabilitation Society of Calgary
7 11th St. N.E.
Calgary, AB T2E 4Z2
Canada
www.members.shaw.ca/reha
bcalgary/rehabcalgary.html

Resource Center for Accessible Living, Inc.
602 Albany Ave.
Kingston, NY 12401
845-331-0541

Riverfront Foundation
3000 South Ave.
La Crosse, WI 54601
608-784-9450
800-949-7380
www.riverfrontinc.com

Rockingham Opportunities
342 Cherokee Camp Rd.
Reidsville, NC 27320
336-342-4761

Sheltered Workshop
P.O. Box 2002
Clarksburg, WV 26302-2002
304-623-3757

Society for Handicapped Citizens
4283 Paradise Rd.
Seville, OH 44273
330-725-7041
330-336-2045

Photo: Jim Jordan

"If you wouldn't wear your dog ... please don't wear any fur."

—Charlize Theron

The only difference between your "best friend" and animals killed for their fur is how we treat them. All animals feel pain and suffer when trappers and farmers break their necks or electrocute them for their pelts. Learn more at **PETA.org**.

PeTA

HEALTH CHARITIES THAT **DON'T FUND** ANIMAL EXPERIMENTS

Southwest Center for Independent Living
2864 S. Nettleton Ave.
Springfield, MO 65807-5970
800-676-7245
www.swcil.org

Specialized Training for Adult Rehabilitation (START)
20 N. 13th St.
Murphysboro, IL 62966-0938
618-687-2378

St. Paul Abilities Network
P.O. Box 457
4915-51 Ave.
St. Paul, AB T0A 3A0
Canada
866-645-3900
www.stpaulabilitiesnetwork.ca

Turn Community Services
P.O. Box 1287
Salt Lake City, UT 84110-1287
866-359-8876

Victor C. Neumann Association
5547 N. Ravenswood St.
Chicago, IL 60640
773-769-4313
www.vcna.org

Vocational Services, Inc. (VSI)
935 Kent St.
Liberty, MO 64068
816-781-6292
www.vsiserve.org

VOLAR Center for Independent Living
8929 Viscount, Ste. 101
El Paso, TX 79225
915-591-0800

Waukesha Training Center
300 S. Prairie
Waukesha, WI 53186
414-547-6821

Western Carolina Center Foundation, Inc.
P.O. Box 646
Morganton, NC 28680-0646
704-433-2862

Workshop/Northeast Career Planning
339 Broadway
Menards, NY 12204
518-463-8051

ELDERLY

Aging & Disabled Services, Inc.
811 S. Palmer Ave.
Box 142
Georgiana, AL 36033

Beth Haven
2500 Pleasant St.
Hannibal, MO 63401
573-221-6000

Carroll County Health and Home Care Services
Carroll County Complex
Ossipee, NH 03864
800-499-4171

DARTS
1645 Marthaler Ln. W.
St. Paul, MN 55118
651-455-1560

Getabout
P.O. Box 224
New Canaan, CT 06840-0224
203-972-7433

Prairie Mission Retirement Village
242 Carroll St.
R.R. 1, Box 1Z
St. Paul, KS 66771
620-449-2400

Royal Freemasons Benevolent Institution of New South Whales
P.O. Box A 2019
Sydney NSW 2000
Australia
011 61 2 9264 5986

Wesley Heights
580 Long Hill Ave.
Shelton, CT 06484
203-929-5396

EMOTIONAL/ BEHAVIORAL DISORDERS

AIMCenter
1903 McCallie Ave.
Chattanooga, TN 37404
423-624-4800

Burke Foundation
20800 Farm Rd. 150 W.
Driftwood, TX 78619
512-858-4258

Crestwood Children's Center
2075 Scottsville Rd.
Rochester, NY 14623-2098
716-436-4442

Federation of Families for Children's Mental Health
1101 King St., Ste. 420
Alexandria, VA 22314
703-684-7710
www.ffcmh.org

Grace House
2412 Tulip
Carlsbad, NM 88220
505-885-3681
www.gracehouse.net

Lake Whatcom Center
3400 Agate Hts.
Bellingham, WA 98226
360-676-6000

**Parents and Children
Coping Together
(PACCT)**
P.O. Box 26691
Richmond, VA 23261-6691
800-477-0946
www.pacct.net

Rimrock Foundation
1231 N. 29th St.
Billings, MT 59101
800-227-3953

**Staten Island Mental
Health Society, Inc.**
669 Castleton Ave.
Staten Island, NY 10301
718-442-2225

**Timberlawn Psychiatric
Research Foundation,
Inc.**
P.O. Box 270789
Dallas, TX 75227-0789
214-338-0451

**TRANSACT Health
Systems of Central
Pennsylvania**
610 Beatty Rd.
Monroeville, PA 15146
814-371-0414

**Youth Services for
Oklahoma County**
21 N.E. 50th St.
Oklahoma City, OK 73105-
1811
405-235-7537

HOME CARE/MEALS

**Bronx Home Care
Services, Inc.**
3956 Bronxwood Ave.
Bronx, NY 10466
718-231-6292

**Greystoke Homes and
Support Services, Inc.**
701 Second Ave. S.
Lethbridge, AB T1J 0C4
Canada
403-320-0911

Mobile Meals, Inc.
1063 S. Broadway
Akron, OH 44311
330-376-7717
800-TLC-MEAL
www.mobilemealsinc.org

Project Open Hand
730 Polk St.
San Francisco, CA 94109
510-596-8200
800-551-MEAL
www.openhand.org

KIDNEY

American Kidney Fund
6110 Executive Blvd.
Ste. 1010
Rockville, MD 20852
800-638-8299
www.kidneyfund.org
✓

MISCELLANEOUS

Action Against Hunger
247 W. 37th St., Ste. 1201
New York, NY 10018
212-967-7800
www.actionagainsthunger.org

**American Fund for
Alternatives to Animal
Research**
175 W. 12th St., Ste. 16G
New York, NY 10011-8220
212-989-8073

**American Hospice
Foundation**
2120 L St. N.W., Ste. 200
Washington, DC 20037
202-223-0204
www.americanhospice.org

**American Leprosy
Missions**
1 ALMWay
Greenville, SC 29601
800-543-3135
www.leprosy.org

**American Vitiligo
Research Foundation,
Inc.**
P.O. Box 7540
Clearwater, FL 33758
727-461-3899
www.avrf.org

**Autism Treatment
Services of
Saskatchewan, Inc.**
2229 Ave. C N.
Saskatoon, SK S7L 5Z2
Canada
306-655-7013
www.autism-atss.com

**Colostomy Society of
New York, G.P.O.**
P.O. Box 517
New York, NY 10016
212-903-4713

HEALTH CHARITIES THAT **DON'T FUND** ANIMAL EXPERIMENTS

Floating Hospital
232 E. Broadway
New York, NY 10002
917-534-0076
www.thefloatinghospital.org

Follow-Your-Heart Foundation
5144 Bascule Ave.
Woodland Hills, CA 91364-3447
818-992-3212
www.followyourheart.org

Giving MD A Voice
5334 Granada Blvd.
Sebring, FL 33872
866-632-8642
www.hopeformd.com

The Healing Hands Project
P.O. Box 1957
Burbank, CA 91507-9998
323-851-2000
www.healinghandsproject.com

Heimlich Institute
P.O. Box 8858
Cincinnati, OH 45208
513-559-2391
www.heimlichinstitute.org

Lions Eye Bank of NW Pa., Inc.
5015 Richmond St.
Erie, PA 16509-1949
814-866-3545

MAWA Trust
66 Oxford St., Ste. 6A
Darlinghurst NSW 2010
Australia
011 61 2 9360 7114

McDougall Research and Education Foundation
P.O. Box 14309
Santa Rose, CA 95402
707-538-8609
www.drmcdougall.com

MCS Referral and Resources (Multiple Chemical Sensitivity)
508 Westgate Rd.
Baltimore, MD 21229-2343
410-362-6400
www.mcsrr.org

MISS Foundation
P.O. Box 5333
Peoria, AZ 85385-5333
623-979-1000
www.missfoundation.org

Multiple Sclerosis Foundation
6350 N. Andrews Ave.
Fort Lauderdale, FL 33309-2130
954-776-6805
www.msfacts.org

National Stuttering Association
119 W. 40th St., 14th Fl.
New York, NY 10018
212-944-4050
www.westutter.org

Naturaleza, Inc.
8889 Mentor Ave.
Mentor, OH 44060
440-796-6319
www.naturalezafoundation

Pride Youth Programs
4684 S. Evergreen
Newaygo, MI 49337
800-668-9277
www.prideyouthprograms.org

Recovery Path Foundation
908 W. Horatio St., Ste. A
Tampa, FL 33606
813-514-0350
www.recoverypathfoundation.org

REMEDY, Inc.
3 TMP, 333 Cedar St.
P.O. Box 208051
New Haven, CT 06520-8051
203-737-5356
www.remedyinc.org

Seva Foundation
1786 Fifth St.
Berkeley, CA 94710
510-845-7382
www.seva.org

Thyroid Society
7515 S. Main St., Ste. 545
Houston, TX 77030
800-THYROID
www.the-thyroid-society.org

Transplantation Society of Michigan
2203 Platt Rd.
Ann Arbor, MI 48104
800-482-4881
www.tsm-giftoflife.org

Vulvar Pain Foundation
P.O. Drawer 177
Graham, NC 27253
336-226-0704
www.vulvarpainfoundation.org

PARALYSIS

**Spinal Cord Injury
Network International**
3911 Princeton Dr.
Santa Rosa, CA 95405
800-548-CORD
www.spinalcordinjury.org

SUBSTANCE ABUSE

**Family Service
Association**
31 W. Market St.
Wilkes-Barre, PA 18701-
1304
570-823-5144

**Friendly Hand
Foundation**
347 S. Normandie Ave.
Los Angeles, CA 90020
213-389-9964

**Prevention of Alcohol
Problems, Inc.**
2125 Glenhaven Ln. N.
Brooklyn Park, MN 55443-
3806
612-729-3047

**Recovery Path
Foundation**
908 W. Horatio St., Ste. A
Tampa, FL 33606
813-514-0350
www.recoverypathfoundatio
n.org

**Samaritan Recovery
Community, Inc.**
319 S. Fourth St.
Nashville, TN 37206
615-244-4802

TRAUMA/INJURY

**Brain Injury Association
of America**
8201 Greensboro Dr.
Ste. 611
McLean, VA 22102
800-444-0755

**Brain Injury Association
of Florida, Inc.**
201 E. Sample Rd.
Pompano Beach, FL 33064
954-786-2400
www.biaf.org

**Brain Injury
Rehabilitation Centre**
300, 815 Eighth Ave. S.W.
Calgary, AB T2P 3P2
Canada
403-297-0100
www.brainrehab.ca

**Trauma Foundation
San Francisco General
Hospital**
Bldg. 1, Rm. 300
1001 Potrero Ave.
San Francisco, CA 94110
415-821-8209
www.tf.org

VETERANS

**Help Hospitalized
Veterans**
36585 Penfield Ln.
Winchester, CA 92596
909-926-4500
www.hhv.org

HEALTH CHARITIES THAT **DO FUND** ANIMAL EXPERIMENTS

What Types of Charities Are on the 'Do Test' List?

Health charities that conduct or fund experiments on animals are included on the "do test" list. These organizations deal with human health issues ranging from lung cancer to drug addiction to blindness. While some do have relevant and effective projects that help improve lives, all of them drain money away from these projects in order to support cruel experiments on animals. They starve, cripple, burn, poison, and cut open animals to study human diseases and disabilities. Such experiments are of no practical benefit to anyone. They are unnecessary, unreliable, and misleading. "Enormous variations exist among rats, rabbits, dogs, pigs, and human beings, and meaningful scientific conclusions cannot be drawn about one species by studying another," says Neal Barnard, M.D. "Non-animal methods provide a more accurate method of testing and can be interpreted more objectively."

What Can Be Done to Stop Charities From Experimenting on Animals?

Many charities know that we can improve treatments through modern, non-animal methods, and they fund only non-animal research, leading to real progress in the prevention and treatment of disease. The next time you receive a donation request from a health charity, ask if it funds animal tests. Write to let charities know that you give only to organizations that alleviate suffering, not to those that contribute to it.

Please note that most colleges and universities have laboratories that conduct animal experiments. If you would like to know if a specific school has an animal laboratory, please contact PETA. For information on the experiments being conducted or to voice your opinion, please contact the school directly.

The following health charities and service organizations conduct or fund animal experiments. They may deal with several issues, including nonhealth-related issues, but they are listed according to their primary health focus. Listed in parentheses are affiliated organizations that may or may not fund animal experiments. For more information on the programs and activities of an organization, please contact the organization directly.

HEALTH CHARITIES THAT **DO FUND** ANIMAL EXPERIMENTS

AIDS

American Foundation for AIDS Research (AMFAR)
733 Third Ave., 12th Fl.
New York, NY 10017
800-39-AMFAR
www.amfar.org

Elizabeth Glaser Pediatric AIDS Foundation
2950 31st St., Ste. 125
Santa Monica, CA 90405
310-314-1459
888-499-4673
www.pedaids.org

Pediatric AIDS Foundation
1311 Colorado Ave.
Santa Monica, CA 90404
310-395-9051

ALZHEIMER'S DISEASE

Alzheimer's Association
919 N. Michigan Ave.
Ste. 1000
Chicago, IL 60611-1676
312-335-8700
800-272-3900
www.alz.org

Alzheimer's Disease Research
(American Health Assistance Foundation)
22512 Gateway Center Dr.
Clarksburg, MD 20871
800-437-AHAF
www.ahaf.org

Alzheimer Society of Canada
20 Eglinton Ave. W.
Ste. 1200
Toronto, ON M4R 1K8
Canada
416-488-8772
www.alzheimer.ca

ARTHRITIS

Arthritis Foundation
1330 W. Peachtree St.
Atlanta, GA 30309
404-872-7100
www.arthritis.org

BIRTH DEFECTS

March of Dimes Birth Defects Foundation
1275 Mamaroneck Ave.
White Plains, NY 10605
914-997-4504
www.modimes.org

Muscular Dystrophy Association
3300 E. Sunrise Dr.
Tucson, AZ 85718-3208
800-572-1717
www.mdausa.org

Shriners Hospitals for Crippled Children
International Shrine Headquarters
2900 Rocky Point Dr.
Tampa, FL 33607
813-281-0300
www.shrinershq.org

The Smile Train
245 Fifth Ave., Ste. 2201
New York, NY 10016
877-543-7645
www.smiletrain.org

United Cerebral Palsy
1660 L St. N.W., Ste. 700
Washington, DC 20036
202-776-0406
www.ucpa.org

BLIND/VISUALLY IMPAIRED

Foundation Fighting Blindness
11435 Cronhill Dr.
Owings Mills, MD 21117-2220
410-568-0150
888-394-3937
www.blindness.org

Macular Degeneration Research
(American Health Assistance Foundation)
22512 Gateway Center Dr.
Clarksburg, MD 20871
800-437-AHAF
www.ahaf.org

Massachusetts Lions Eye Research Fund
(Lions Clubs International Foundation)
118 Allen St.
Hampden, MA 01036
413-566-3756
www.mler.com

National Glaucoma Research
(American Health Assistance Foundation)
22512 Gateway Center Dr.
Clarksburg, MD 20871
800-437-AHAF
www.ahaf.org

Research to Prevent Blindness
645 Madison Ave., 21st Fl.
New York, NY 10022-1010
800-621-0026
www.rpbusa.org

BLOOD

American Red Cross
2025 E. St., N.W.
Washington, DC 20006
202-303-4498
800-435-7669
www.redcross.org

Aplastic Anemia & MDS International Foundation, Inc.
P.O. Box 316
Annapolis, MD 21404-0613
800-747-2820
www.aamds-international.org

Canadian Blood Services
1800 Alta Vista
Ottawa, ON K1G 4J5
Canada
613-739-2300
www.bloodservices.ca

Leukemia & Lymphoma Society of America
1311 Mamaroneck Ave.
White Plains, NY 10605
800-955-4572
www.leukemia.org

National Hemophilia Foundation
116 W. 32nd St., 11th Fl.
New York, NY 10001
212-219-8180
800-42-HANDI
www.hemophilia.org

BURNS

Shriners Burn Institute
International Shrine
Headquarters
2900 Rocky Point Dr.
Tampa, FL 33607
813-281-0300
www.shrinershq.org

CANCER

American Cancer Society
1599 Clifton Rd. N.E.
Atlanta, GA 30329
404-320-3333
www.cancer.org

American Institute for Cancer Research
1759 R St. N.W.
Washington, DC 20009
202-328-7744
800-843-8114
www.aicr.org

Arizona Cancer Center
1515 N. Campbell Ave.
P.O. Box 245013
Tucson, AZ 85724-5013
520-626-5279
800-327-CURE
www.azcc.arizona.edu

The Breast Cancer Research Foundation
654 Madison Ave., Ste. 1209
New York, NY 10021
646-497-2600
www.bcrfcure.org

British Columbia Cancer Foundation
200-601 W. Broadway
Vancouver, BC V5Z 4C2
Canada
888-906-2873
www.bccancerfoundation.com

Canadian Cancer Society/National Cancer Institute of Canada
10 Alcorn Ave., Ste. 200
Toronto, ON M4V 3B1
Canada
416-961-7223
www.cancer.ca
www.ncic.cancer.ca

Cancer Research Foundation of America
1600 Duke St., Ste. 110
Alexandria, VA 22314
703-836-4412
800-227-2732
www.preventcancer.org

The Cancer Research Society, Inc.
402-625 Av Du President
Kennedy
Montreal QC H3A 3S5
Canada
514-861-9227
www.CancerResearchSociety.ca

Children's Cancer Research Fund
4930 W. 77th St., Ste. 364
Minneapolis, MN 55435
952-893-9355
800-4CCRF48
www.childrenscancer.com

City of Hope
1500 E. Duarte Rd.
Duarte, CA 91010
626-359-8111
www.cityofhope.org

Dana-Farber Cancer Institute
375 Longwood Ave.
Boston, MA 02215
800-253-6667
www.dfci.harvard.edu

Fred Hutchinson Cancer Research Center
1100 Fairview Ave., N.
P.O. Box 19024
Seattle, WA 98109
206-667-5000
www.fhcrc.org

HEALTH CHARITIES THAT **DO FUND** ANIMAL EXPERIMENTS

G & P Foundation for Cancer Research
770 Lexington Ave., 17th Fl.
New York, NY 10021-8165
212-486-2575
www.gpcharity.com

The Jimmy Fund
171 Dwight Rd.
Long Meadow, MA 01106
413-567-0651
www.jimmyfund.org

John Wayne Cancer Institute
2200 Santa Monica Blvd.
Santa Monica, CA 90404
310-315-6111
800-262-6259
www.jwci.org

Lance Armstrong Foundation
P.O. Box 161150
Austin, TX 78716-1150
512-236-8820
www.laf.org

Leukemia & Lymphoma Society of America
1311 Mamaroneck Ave.
White Plains, NY 10605
800-955-4572
www.leukemia.org

Leukemia Research Fund of Canada
110 Finch Ave. W., Ste. 220
Toronto, ON M3J 2T2
Canada
800-268-2144
www.leukemia.ca

Lombardi Cancer Center
3970 Reservoir Rd. N.W.
Washington, DC 20007
202-687-2956
www.lombardi.georgetown.edu

Memorial Sloan-Kettering Cancer Center
1275 York Ave.
New York, NY 10021
212-639-2000
www.mskcc.org

National Cancer Research Center
18 N. Law St.
Aberdeen, MD 21001-2443
410-272-0775

National Colorectal Cancer Research Alliance
(Entertainment Industry Foundation)
1132 Ventura Blvd., #401
Studio City, CA 91604
818-760-7722
www.eifoundation.org

National Foundation for Cancer Research
4600 East-West Hwy.
Ste. 525
Bethesda, MD 20814
800-321-2873
www.nfcr.org

National Women's Cancer Research Alliance
(Entertainment Industry Foundation)
11132 Ventura Blvd., #401
Studio City, CA 91604
818-760-7722
www.eifoundation.org

Nina Hyde Center for Breast Cancer Research, Lombardi Cancer Research Center
3800 Reservoir Rd. N.W.
Washington, DC 20007
202-687-4597

The Ovarian Cancer Research Fund
One Penn Plz., Ste. 1610
New York, NY 10119
212-268-1002
800-873-9569
www.ocrf.org

Pancreatic Cancer Action Network
2221 Rosecrans Ave.
Ste.131
El Segundo, CA 90245
310-725-0025
877-272-6226
www.pancan.org

St. Jude Children's Research Hospital
501 St. Jude Pl.
Memphis, TN 38105
901-495-3300
www.stjude.org

Susan G. Komen Breast Cancer Foundation
5005 LBJ Fwy., Ste. 370
Dallas, TX 75244
972-855-1600
800-462-9273
www.komen.org

Terry Fox Foundation
60 St. Clair Ave. E., Ste. 605
Toronto, ON M4T 1N5
Canada
416-962-7866
www.terryfoxrun.org

The V Foundation for Cancer Research
100 Towerview Ct.
Cary, NC 27513
919-380-9505
800-4-JIMMYV
www.jimmyv.org

CARDIOVASCULAR

American Heart Association
7272 Greenville Ave.
Dallas, TX 75231-4596
214-373-6300
800-AHA-USA1
www.americanheart.org

Heart and Stroke Foundation of Canada
222 Queen St., Ste. 1402
Ottawa, ON K1P 5V9
Canada
613-569-4361
www.hsf.ca

National Cardiovascular Research Initiative
(Entertainment Industry Foundation)
11132 Ventura Blvd., #401
Studio City, CA 91604
818-760-7722
www.eifoundation.org

National Heart Foundation
(American Health Assistance Foundation)
22512 Gateway Center Dr.
Clarksburg, MD 20871
800-437-AHAF
www.ahaf.org

National Stroke Association
9707 E. Easter Ln.
Englewood, CO 80112
800-STROKES
www.strokes.org

CHILDREN

BC Children's Hospital Foundation
4480 Oak St., Rm. B321
Vancouver, BC V6H 3V4
Canada
888-663-3033
www.bcchf.ca

Boys Town National Research Hospital
555 N. 30th St.
Omaha, NE 68131
402-498-6511
www.boystown.org

Children's Cancer Research Fund
4930 W. 77th St., Ste. 364
Minneapolis, MN 55435
952-893-9355
800-4CCRF48
www.childrenscancer.com

Children's Hospital of Pittsburgh Foundation
3705 Fifth Ave.
Pittsburgh, PA 15213-2583
412-692-7436
www.chp.edu

Children's Miracle Network
4525 S. 2300 E.
Ste. 202
Salt Lake City, UT 84117
801-278-8900
801-277-8787
www.cmn.org

Children's National Medical Center
1630 Columbia Rd., N.W.
Washington, DC 20009-3602
888-884-2327
www.cnmc.org

Elizabeth Glaser Pediatric AIDS Foundation
2950 31st St., Ste. 125
Santa Monica, CA 90405
310-314-1459
888-499-4673
www.pedaids.org

The Jimmy Fund
171 Dwight Rd.
Long Meadow, MA 01106
413-567-0651
www.jimmyfund.org

Johns Hopkins Children's Center
One Charles Ctr.
100 N. Charles St., Ste. 200
Baltimore, MD 21201
410-516-4581
www.hopkinschildrens.org

Juvenile Diabetes Research Foundation International (JDRF)
120 Wall St.
New York, NY 10005-4001
800-JDF-CURE
www.jdfcure.com

Pediatric AIDS Foundation
1311 Colorado Ave.
Santa Monica, CA 90404
310-395-9051

Shriners Hospitals for Crippled Children, International Shrine Headquarters
2900 Rocky Point Dr.
Tampa, FL 33607
813-281-0300
www.shrinershq.org

The Smile Train
245 Fifth Ave., Ste. 2201
New York, NY 10016
877-543-7645
www.smiletrain.org

Society for Pediatric Pathology
3643 Walton Way Extension
Augusta, GA 30909
706-364-3375
www.spponline.org

HEALTH CHARITIES THAT **DO FUND** ANIMAL EXPERIMENTS

**St. Jude Children's
Research Hospital**
501 St. Jude Pl.
Memphis, TN 38105
901-495-3300
www.stjude.org

**Sudden Infant Death
Syndrome Alliance**
1314 Bedford Ave.
Ste. 210
Baltimore, MD 21208
800-221-SIDS
www.sidsalliance.org

DEAF/HEARING IMPAIRED

**Boys Town National
Research Hospital**
555 N. 30th St.
Omaha, NE 68131
402-498-6511
www.boystown.org

**Deafness Research
Foundation**
1050 17th St. N.W., Ste. 701
Washington, DC 20036
202-289-5850
www.drf.org

DIABETES

**American Diabetes
Association**
1701 N. Beauregard St.
Alexandria, VA 22311
703-549-1500
800-342-2383
www.diabetes.org

**Canadian Diabetes
Association**
National Life Building
1400-522 University Ave.
Toronto, ON M5G 2R5
Canada
416-363-0177
800-226-8464
www.diabetes.ca

Joslin Diabetes Center
One Joslin Pl.
Boston, MA 02215
617-732-2400
www.joslin.harvard.edu

**Juvenile Diabetes
Foundation
International**
120 Wall St.
New York, NY 10005-4001
800-JDF-CURE
www.jdfcure.com

ELDERLY

**American Federation
for Aging Research**
70 W. 40th St., 11th Fl.
New York, NY 10018
212-703-9977
888-582-2327
www.afar.org

EMOTIONAL/ BEHAVIORAL DISORDERS

**National Alliance for
Research of
Schizophrenia and
Depression**
60 Cutter Mill Rd., Ste. 404
Great Neck, NY 11021
516-829-0091
800-829-8289
www.narsad.org

**National Alliance for the
Mentally Ill**
Colonial Place Three
2107 Wilson Blvd., Ste. 300
Arlington, VA 22201
703-524-7600
www.nami.org

EPILEPSY

**Epilepsy Foundation of
America**
4351 Garden City Dr.
Ste. 500
Landover, MD 20785
301-459-3700
www.efa.org

KIDNEY

**The Kidney Foundation
of Canada**
15 Gervais Dr., Ste. 700
Toronto, ON M3C 1Y8
Canada
800-378-4474
www.kidneycob.on.ca

**National Kidney
Foundation**
30 E. 33rd St., Ste. 1100
New York, NY 10016
212-889-2210
800-622-9010
www.kidney.org

LUNG

**American Lung
Association**
1740 Broadway
New York, NY 10019
212-315-8700
www.lungusa.org

**British Columbia Lung
Association**
2675 Oak St.
Vancouver, BC V6H 2K2
Canada
604-731-5864
www.bc.lung.ca

MISCELLANEOUS

Alliance for Lupus Research, Inc.
1270 Ave. of the Americas,
Ste. 609
New York, NY 10020
212-218-2840
www.lupusresearch.org

American Brain Tumor Association
2727 River Rd., Ste. 146
Des Plains, IL 60018-4110
800-886-2282
www.abta.org

American Digestive Health Foundation
7910 Woodmont Ave.
Ste. 700
Bethesda, MD 20814-3015
301-654-2635

American Health Assistance Foundation
15825 Shady Grove Rd.
Ste. 140
Rockville, MD 20850
800-437-2423
www.ahaf.org

American Liver Foundation
75 Maiden Ln., Ste. 603
New York, NY 10038
800-465-4837
www.liverfoundation.org

American Tinnitus Association
P.O. Box 5
Portland, OR 97207-0005
503-248-9985
800-634-8978
www.ata.org

Amyotrophic Lateral Sclerosis Association (ALS)
27001 Agoura Rd., Ste. 150
Calabasas Hills, CA 91301-5104
818-880-9007
www.alsa.org

Amyotrophic Lateral Sclerosis (ALS) Society of Canada
265 Yorkland Blvd., Ste. 300
Toronto, ON M2J 1S5
Canada
800-267-4257
www.als.ca

BNI Foundation
350 W. Thomas Rd.
Phoenix, AZ 85013
602-406-3041

Canadian Cystic Fibrosis Foundation
2221 Yonge St., Ste. 601
Toronto, ON M4S 2B4
Canada
800-378-2233
www.cysticfibrosis.ca

Canadian Hemophilia Society
625 President Kennedy Ave.
Ste. 1210
Montreal, QC H3A 1K2
Canada
800-668-2686
www.hemophilia.ca

Charcot-Marie-Tooth Association
2700 Chestnut St.
Chester, PA 19013-4867
800-606-CMTA
www.charcot-marie-tooth.org

Crohn's & Colitis Foundation of America
386 Park Ave. S.
New York, NY 10016-8804
800-932-2423
www.ccfa.org

Cure Autism Now
5455 Wilshire Blvd., Ste. 715
Los Angeles, CA 90036-4234
888-828-8476
www.cureautismnow.org

Cystic Fibrosis Foundation
6931 Arlington Rd.
Bethesda, MD 20814
800-FIGHT-CF
www.cff.org

Endometriosis Association
8585 N. 76th Pl.
Milwaukee, WI 53223
414-355-2200
800-992-3636
www.endometriosisassn.org

Entertainment Industry Foundation
11132 Ventura Blvd. #401
Studio City, CA 91604
818-760-7722
www.eifoundation.org

Families of Spinal Muscular Atrophy
P.O. Box 196
Libertyville, IL 60048-0196
800-886-1762
www.fsma.org

Fonds de la Recherche en Santé du Québec
500 Rue, Sherbrooke Quest
Bureau 800
Montreal QC H3A 3C6
Canada
514-873-2114
www.frsq.gouv.qc.ca

HEALTH CHARITIES THAT **DO FUND** ANIMAL EXPERIMENTS

Huntington's Disease Society of America
158 W. 29th St., 7th Fl.
New York, NY 10001-5300
800-345-HDSA
www.hdsa.org

Life Extension Foundation
P.O. Box 229120
Hollywood, FL 33022-9120
800-544-4440
www.lef.org

Lupus Foundation of America
1300 Piccard Dr., Ste. 200
Rockville, MD 20850-4303
800-558-0121
www.lupus.org

Multiple Sclerosis Society of Canada
175 Bloor St. E., Ste. 700
Toronto, ON M4W 3R8
Canada
800-268-7582
www.mssociety.ca

National Headache Foundation
428 W. St. James Pl., 2nd Fl.
Chicago, IL 60614-2750
800-NHF-5552
www.headaches.org

National Jewish Medical and Research Center
1400 Jackson St.
Denver, CO 80206
303-388-4461
www.nationaljewish.org

National Multiple Sclerosis Society
733 Third Ave., 6th Fl.
New York, NY 10017-3288
800-344-4867
www.nmss.org

National Osteoporosis Foundation
1232 22nd St. N.W.
Washington, DC 20037-1292
202-223-2226
www.nof.org

National Psoriasis Foundation
6600 S.W. 92nd Ave., Ste. 300
Portland, OR 97223-7195
503-244-7404
800-723-9166
www.psoriasis.org

National Vitiligo Foundation
611 S. Fleishel Ave.
Tyler, TX 75701
903-531-0074
www.nvfi.org

Natural Sciences and Engineering Research Council of Canada
350 Albert St.
Ottawa, ON K1A 1H5
Canada
613-992-0842

Plastic Surgery Education Foundation/American Society of Plastic and Reconstructive Surgery (PSEF/ASPS)
444 E. Algonquin Rd.
Arlington Heights, IL 60005
847-228-9900

Project A.L.S.
511 Ave. of the Americas
PMB #341
New York, NY 10011
800-603-0270
www.projectals.org

Schizophrenia Society of Canada
50 Acadia Ave., Ste. 205
Markham, ON L3R 0B3
Canada
905-415-2007
www.schizophrenia.ca

Stem Cell Research Foundation
22512 Gateway Center Dr.
Clarksburg, MD 20871
877-842-3442
www.stemcellresearchfoundation.org

Sunnybrook & Women's Foundation
2075 Bayview Ave.
Toronto, ON M4N 3M5
Canada
416-480-4483
www.sunnybrookandwomens.on.ca

Tourette Syndrome Association
42-40 Bell Blvd.
Bayside, NY 11361-2820
718-224-2999
800-237-0717
www.tsa-usa.org

PARALYSIS

American Paralysis Foundation
500 Morris Ave.
Springfield, NJ 07081
201-379-2690

The Buoniconti Fund
P.O. Box 016960, R-48
Miami, FL 33101
305-243-6001

Christopher Reeve Paralysis Foundation
500 Morris Ave.
Springfield, NJ 07081
800-225-0292
www.christopherreeve.org

**Eastern Paralyzed
Veterans Association**
75-20 Astoria Blvd.
Jackson Heights, NY 11370
718-803-3782
www.unitedspinal.org

**Miami Project to Cure
Paralysis**
P.O. Box 016960, R-48
Miami, FL 33101
305-243-6001
www.miamiproject.miami.edu

**Paralyzed Veterans of
America**
801 18th St. N.W.
Washington, DC 20006-
3715
202-872-1300
800-424-8200
www.pva.org

**United Spinal
Association**
75-20 Astoria Blvd.
Jackson Heights, NY 11370
718-803-3782
www.unitedspinal.org

**PARKINSON'S
DISEASE**

**American Parkinson
Disease Association**
1250 Hylan Blvd., Ste. 4B
Staten Island, NY 10305
800-223-2732
www.apdaparkinson.com

**Michael J. Fox
Foundation for
Parkinson's Research**
Grand Central Station
P.O. Box 4777
New York, NY 10163
707-544-1994
www.michaeljfox.org

**National Parkinson
Foundation**
1501 N.W. Ninth Ave.
Miami, FL 33136
800-327-4545
www.parkinson.org

**Parkinson's Disease
Foundation, Inc.**
710 W. 168th St.
New York, NY 10032-9982
212-923-4700
800-457-6676
www.pdf.org

VETERANS

**Paralyzed Veterans of
America**
801 18th St. N.W.
Washington, DC 20006-
3715
202-872-1300
800-424-8200
www.pva.org

**United Spinal
Association**
75-20 Astoria Blvd.
Jackson Heights, NY 11370
718-803-3782
www.unitedspinal.org

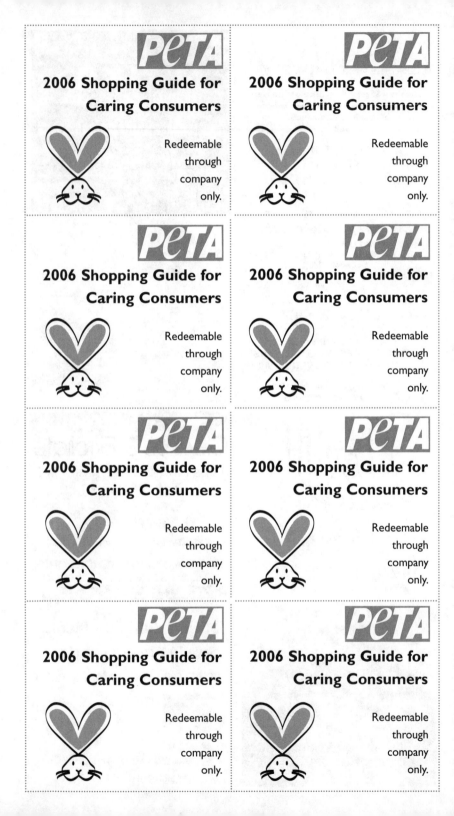

fetch

a dog from a shelter, **not** from a pet store

This puppy will pay
with her life if you
buy from a pet store.
When you buy,
a pound puppy will die.

WHAT IS **PETA?**

People for the Ethical Treatment of Animals (PETA) is an international nonprofit organization dedicated to exposing and eliminating the abuse of animals. PETA uses public education, litigation, research and investigations, media campaigns, and involvement at the grassroots level to accomplish this goal.

With the help of our dedicated members, PETA persuades major corporations to stop testing products on animals, advocates alternatives to eating animals by promoting a vegan diet, and has forced the closure of federally funded animal-research facilities because of animal abuse.

To help stop the exploitation and abuse of animals, become a PETA member today.

MEMBERSHIP & DONATION FORM

Enclosed is my contribution to assist your vital work in behalf of all animals.

❏ $16   ❏ $25   ❏ $50   ❏ $100   ❏ Other $_____

(Annual membership is $16. Members receive The PETA Guide to Compassionate Living and a subscription to PETA's quarterly magazine.)

❏ I'm already a PETA member. This is an additional donation.

Name _____

Address _____

City_____ State _____ Zip_____

E-Mail: _____

Complete this form and send with your check to:

 PEOPLE FOR THE ETHICAL TREATMENT OF ANIMALS
501 Front St., Norfolk, VA 23510

Thank you from all of us at PETA.

cguide